MISSION
IN THE
NINETEEN
90s

This edition first published 1991 jointly by
Wm. B. Eerdmans Publishing Co.
255 Jefferson Ave. SE, Grand Rapids, MI 49503
and
Overseas Ministries Study Center
490 Prospect St., New Haven, CT 06511.

Printed in the United States of America

Library of Congress Cataloging in Publication Data

Mission in the nineteen 90s / edited by Gerald H. Anderson, James M. Phillips,
    Robert T. Coote; contributors: Arthur F. Glasser . . . [et al.].
        p.   cm.
    ISBN 0-8028-0542-6
    1. Missions.   I. Anderson, Gerald H.   II. Phillips, James M., 1929-   .
III. Coote, Robert T., 1932-   . IV. Glasser, Arthur F. (Arthur Frederick),
1914-   . V. Title: Mission in the 1990s.
BV2070.M556   1991
266—dc20   90-23260
                                                                              CIP

Design by Robin Heller

International Bulletin
of Missionary Research

P R E S E N T S

MISSION
IN THE
NINETEEN
90s

Edited by

Gerald H. Anderson   James M. Phillips   Robert T. Coote

Arthur F. Glasser
Michael Amaladoss, S.J.
Johannes Verkuyl
Anna Marie Aagaard
Lesslie Newbigin

Barbara Hendricks, M.M.
C. René Padilla
Desmond M. Tutu
Neuza Itioka
C. G. Arévalo, S.J.
Bishop Anastasios

Ralph D. Winter
Mary Motte, F.M.M.
Emilio Castro
David J. Bosch
L. Grant McClung, Jr.
David B. Barrett

WILLIAM B. EERDMANS PUBLISHING COMPANY
GRAND RAPIDS, MICHIGAN

OVERSEAS MINISTRIES STUDY CENTER
NEW HAVEN, CONNECTICUT

CONTENTS

The Evangelicals: Unwavering Commitment, Troublesome Divisions

Arthur F. Glasser

In the closing decade of the twentieth century, evangelicals will play a major role. In this article we shall attempt to describe their missionary involvement and to suggest where they will be at the end of the century. This is a daunting assignment; I can only plead the apostle Paul's caution, namely, that we see dimly, having only partial knowledge (1 Cor. 13:12).

Evangelicals have a growing awareness of their size and strength. They have much empirical evidence to bolster the venturesome elan currently surging through their ranks. At the same time, some of their leaders fear that the worldwide evangelical community could lose its spiritual cohesion if certain troublesome issues are not satisfactorily resolved.

But who are these people? Evangelicals represent a movement that defies precise definition. They do not constitute a particular institution, but rather, an amorphous movement that exists in practically every Protestant tradition within the worldwide Christian church, a movement having a religious identity characterized by the term "evangelicalism." Years ago Max Warren, then leader of the Church Missionary Society, offered a helpful definition of evangelicalism when he said (1962, p. 1) that it consists of "a particular balance" in the following cluster of biblical themes: (1) unquestioned submission to the trustworthiness and authority of Scripture as the Word of God; (2) the essentiality of the atonement of Christ; (3) an existential saving encounter with the Holy Spirit; and (4) a concern for the proper, scriptural use of the sacraments. Most evangelicals would add the obligation to evangelize non-Christians throughout the world.

Theological Non-Negotiables

The intensity with which evangelicals adhere to these theological

Arthur F. Glasser is Dean Emeritus, School of World Mission, Fuller Theological Seminary, Pasadena, California. He was a missionary to China, 1946–51, with China Inland Mission, and later was home director for Overseas Missionary Fellowship in the U.S.A.

postulates should not be underestimated. They are not negotiable. As a result we can confidently predict that in the next decade there will be no erosion of commitment from an unqualified acceptance of Chalcedonian Christology. Evangelicals bow to the mystery of the incarnation of the pre-existent Son of God. Jesus of Nazareth is both *vere Deus* and *vere Homo*. He possesses all that makes God, God— and all that makes man, man. There is no possibility of modifying this Christology in the direction of the speculations of John Hick, Paul Knitter, Norman Pittenger, and so forth. Evangelicals hold, and will continue to hold, all the implications of Paul's witness to Jesus: "Though he was rich, yet for our sakes he became poor, so that by his poverty we might become rich" (2 Cor. 8:9). "He is the image of the invisible God, the firstborn of all creation; for in him all things were created, in heaven and on earth, visible and invisible, whether thrones or dominions or principalities or authorities—all things were created through him and for him" (Col. 1:15–16). Evangelicals affirm the confession of Thomas before the risen Christ: "My Lord and my God!" (Jn. 20:23), and treasure the response of the Savior: "Have you believed because you have seen me? Blessed are those who have not seen and yet believe" (20:29).

> **The intensity with which evangelicals adhere to these theological postulates should not be underestimated.**

Because of evangelical commitment to Scripture and to its unwavering witness to Jesus of Nazareth as the Christ of God, we can confidently state that in the 1990s and beyond, evangelicals will not waver or deviate on two touchstone issues: evangelistic concern for the Jewish people, and the uniqueness of Christ in the midst of religious pluralism. We begin by examining these two unalterables.

Witness to the Jews

The days ahead will mark a steady enlargement of the evangelical witness to the Jewish community worldwide concerning Jesus of Nazareth, the Servant Messiah of Israel and the Savior of the world. Recent steps taken in England to strengthen the Anglican Church's Ministry to the Jews (CMJ, already 179 years old) and the formation of CMJ/USA in 1982 are cases in point. This agency is actively promoting the formation of Messianic Jewish gatherings as well as encouraging Jewish believers in Jesus to enrich the life, worship, and witness of the American Episcopal communion. It is only one among more than sixty evangelical groups in America so engaged.

This evangelical witness to the Jews raises two fundamental biblical issues. First, who is Jesus of Nazareth? What of his claims for himself and the messianic signs that accompanied his ministry? Second, what does the Old Testament promise? One cannot read the law, the prophets, and the writings without entering into the yearning of its writers for the coming of a universal faith for all peoples, centered in the worship of the God of Abraham, Isaac, and Jacob and provided by a son of David. This faith has its rootage in the universal dimensions of the Abrahamic covenant and will be expressed by the realities uniquely revealed at Sinai and never rescinded. Only the New Testament in its fullness reveals the Davidic

Savior and fulfills the yearning for this universal faith. Increasingly Jews are being drawn to these actualities, and the evangelical witness to the Jewish people will steadily increase in the days ahead.

Religious Pluralism

This brings us to the growing phenomenon of religious pluralism. Throughout the world today and increasingly in the days ahead, every city is the locus of competing truth claims and radically diverse answers to the universal religious quest of people. Paul Knitter argues that Christians should settle for a "unitive pluralism of all religions"; they should be polite enough to regard all other religions with respectful good grace and work for tolerant coexistence. Christians should be done with championing and propagating their own particular understanding of truth. But evangelicals will never buy this line, no matter how persuasively it is advanced. Friedrich Schleiermacher interjected into the stream of human thought the concept of comparative religions and regarded the Christian faith as just one of the religions. In contrast, evangelicals point without apology to the mighty acts of God in history: the call of Abraham and the covenant God made with him; the deliverance from Egyptian bondage of his descendants; the Mosaic economy established with them; and the subsequent acts and words whereby God revealed the divine self and the divine universal purpose—all this culminating in the incarnation, death, and resurrection of Jesus, the Messiah of Israel, the Savior of the world, and the eternal Son of God.

Emil Brunner dismissed as utterly untenable the popular opinion that the biblical witness to this divine disclosure has its parallels in other religions (apart from the initial shaping of Judaism as recorded in the Old Testament). He contends:

> The claim of the revelation [by a Revealer] possessing universal validity in the history of religion is rare. The claim of revelation made by the Christian faith is in its radicalization as solitary as its content: the message of atonement. . . . Only at one place, only in one event has God revealed himself truly and completely—there, namely, where he became man. . . . No other religion can assert revelation in the radical unconditional sense in which the Christian faith does this, because no other religion knows the God who is himself the Revealer [1946, pp. 235–36].

It is the uniqueness of the truth claims of biblical Christianity that evangelicals regard as non-negotiable. Regardless of how religiously plural their communities and countries become, evangelicals will continue to regard the essence of their faith as the unique revelation of God, equally valid for all peoples.

And yet there is reason for concern. On one hand, religious pluralism constantly tempts evangelicals to isolate themselves from positive encounter with people of other faiths. On the other hand, they can also become so involved in the crucial task of furthering social harmony in their communities that they find themselves drawing back from the priority of bearing public witness to the scandal of the cross, the essentiality of conversion, and the pursuit of "holiness without which no one will see the Lord" (Heb. 12:14). One can already see too many within the evangelical community tolerating a growing ethical reductionism, which in time cannot but secularize lifestyle and blunt their struggle to manifest their true nature as the redeemed people of God.

My fear also is that with the weakening of the social fabric due to the growth of religious pluralism, evangelicals may grow increasingly fearful of the nation in which they dwell; this applies especially to evangelicals in the United States. Whereas, as stated above, many may drift into materialism and hedonism, others may be seduced by appeals to national security and embrace whatever trappings of civil religion may be advocated to further national cohesion. Evangelicals did not do very well in resisting the blandishments of Hitler's racist and anticommunist religiosity or in opposing Japan's state Shinto. Whereas in their heart of hearts they may have clung to faith in Jesus Christ, their outward lives revealed little evidence of his lordship. Karl Barth said about Psalm 115:46 ("I will also speak of thy testimonies before Kings, and shall not be put to shame") that if the German Church had believed this and obeyed it, Germany would not have gone Nazi.

The Walls within Evangelicalism

Thus far we have assumed that evangelicalism is a monolith by virtue of its unwavering commitment to the authority of Scripture, the deity and humanity of Jesus of Nazareth, the centrality of the atonement, and the essentiality of conversion through linkage

> **It is the uniqueness of the truth claims of biblical Christianity that evangelicals regard as non-negotiable.**

with the Holy Spirit. But on other levels it is exceedingly complex. Robert Webber is convinced that there are at least fourteen major evangelical subcultures and makes no attempt to number the smaller groups within them (1978, p. 32). Although I recognize the futility of trying to define neat categories of classification, one cannot detail the probable trends of their varied missionary outreach in the next decade without identifying the dominant characteristics of the major divisions among them. I shall attempt a fivefold classification. First, the "separatist fundamentalists," many of whom are still in the trenches of the fundamentalist-liberal struggles of the 1920s and 1930s, with their hostilities currently focused on the World Council of Churches (WCC) and all evangelicals in contact with it. They also are anticharismatic. Second, the "low-key dispensational evangelicals" who fight shy of ecumenical encounter, find charismatics a problem, but fill the ranks of both the independent "faith" missions and those of some smaller evangelical denominations (e.g., the Conservative Baptist Association and the Christian and Missionary Alliance). Third, the "charismatic evangelicals" whose groupings range from traditional Pentecostals to the newer mainline charismatics. Not a few tensions exist among them: charismatics are burdened to bring renewal to all churches whether within or outside the WCC, and whether Catholic or Protestant. In contrast, Pentecostals tend to feel that these charismatics have not "gone all the way" in their pursuit of life in the Spirit. Generally speaking, these ardent Christians are outdistancing all other evangelicals in growth and vitality.

Fourth, the "ecumenical evangelicals." This group is struggling to maintain balance between word and power—the two components of the gospel (1 Cor. 2:1–5). They are open to the positive values of critical scholarship and feel obligated to pursue ecumenical relations because of the biblical mandate to promote renewal and to express the unity of "the One, Holy, Catholic and Apostolic Church." They are also concerned to stimulate the social responsibility of all evangelicals. Their numbers are steadily growing, although they are often attacked by the more conservative members of the other evangelical subgroups.

Finally, the "nonconciliar orthodox evangelicals" whose historic roots are so highly cherished that the dominant thrust of their concern is to preserve these values, whether Reformed or Lutheran or Mennonite or Plymouth Brethren. They tend to be ingrown, having largely lost the concern for the renewal of the larger church that originally brought them to birth.

Unfortunately, the distinctives among various evangelical groupings all too often have been accompanied by the erection of walls. As with all walls, they both include and exclude. And there are always the irregulars who ask, "Are these walls necessary?"

Lausanne Committee

The most significant entity for bringing together the varied groups of evangelicals is the Lausanne Committee for World Evangelization (LCWE). It takes as its focus the long-sought goal of evangelicals—that throughout the world wherever there are people, there should be both Christians and structured congregations. LCWE came into existence following the International Congress on World Evangelization, held in Lausanne, Switzerland, in 1974—a massive gathering of almost 4,000 people drawn from 150 nations and representing, though not officially, over 135 denominations. It marked the first time such varied evangelicals faced together the need to express themselves as belonging to a radically different community—a counterculture—scattered by God throughout the nations and obligated by God to be done with self-satisfied triumphalism. They should repent that at that late hour in the history of the church such a massive unfinished missionary task should still await the Christian movement. Their expressed determination was to be done with the old classification of missionary-sending and missionary-receiving countries—the Great Commission applies equally to all Christians everywhere. Here evangelicals were reminded that they should not drive a wedge between their evangelistic outreach and their social responsibilities. They must be done with cultural imperialism and missionary paternalism. People are not to be manipulated. Spiritual results cannot be programmed. One slogan was "integrity and authenticity are far more important than statistics and publicity." Without the love of God flowing forth from one's heart and the evangelistic activity of the Holy Spirit given its rightful place, all efforts are meaningless and futile. As the evangelical leader John Capon reported: "July 1974 saw the emergence of the Lausanne person—a new breed of evangelical, committed to genuinely biblical evangelism, radical discipleship, intense social involvement, sacrificial living, mature partnership and authentic faith." (Crusade, an English periodical, 1974).

In the years since 1974 the fear that LCWE might become a counter World Council of Churches has not materialized. Rather, many LCWE leaders remain loyal members of WCC-related denominations while furthering LCWE concerns. Since the first Lausanne Congress, LCWE has convened a wide range of study conferences and produced an extensive literature on varied themes all supportive of its dominant rubrics: "Let the earth hear his voice" and "How shall they hear?" In July 1989, the LCWE will convene a second major congress, "Lausanne II in Manila," with more than 4000 in attendance, focusing on the theme "Proclaim Christ Until He Comes: A Call to the Whole Church to Take the Whole Gospel to the Whole World."

Unity or Fragmentation?

Lausanne's leaders are not unaware that the fundamental tension among evangelicals is between traditional nonconciliars and the more recent charismatics. This tension could be explosive. The former tend to focus on the "Word of the Cross" while the latter stress the "Power of the Spirit." Both groups are incomplete, needing the balance that comes when both "word" and "power" are rightly related. Tension arises when they face the larger church. The nonconciliars are strongly shaped by an eschatology that keeps before them "the final apostasy." In earlier days they were drilled to believe that the WCC's theological aberrations were but indicators of "the beginning of the end." In contrast, the newer charismatics are sure that they have been brought to the kingdom for such a time as this—to promote renewal and check the secular humanism that has invaded the older churches. They can point to tens of thousands of new churches in North America that have emerged during the past thirty years (estimates range from 70,000 to 100,000 independent renewal congregations in the United States alone). And one thesis continually occupies their concern: evangelicals must work together to bring renewal to every segment of the church, or the evangelization of this generation will not be realized. Some might question their penchant for multiplying structures to accomplish this. Is it not a sign of spiritual anarchy? In one sense, however, this confirms Kenneth Scott Latourette's observation that such activity is an indication of spiritual vitality.

But suppose a charismatic leader had read a recent issue of *Theological News*, (1988, pp. 2–3), the organ of the World Evangelical Fellowship (WEF). It is the WEF to which the great majority of traditional evangelicals belong. Our charismatic leader finds that Theodore Williams, the WEF president, has rejected the idea of "cooperative efforts" with the WCC, since "we should never say social concern and evangelism are equal partners," for "very often [when they are] evangelism and church building are the casualties." Furthermore, he says, the WEF must maintain its "cautious stand with regard to the Roman Catholic Church as long as Rome does not basically change." Then the clincher: the WEF insists that whereas the charismatic movement "brings some life into dead congregations," a warning must be sounded: there is a "great danger, when the charismatic movement does not submit to the Scriptures, and emphasizes personal experience."

What impressions will our charismatic leader gain from these three pronouncements? That at its organizational heart, the WEF is suspicious of charismatics and doesn't really believe in church renewal; it does not expect that prayer and biblical witness, coupled with the activity of the Holy Spirit, will significantly influence either WCC churches or the Roman Catholic Church. It is almost a futile exercise to seek to help them. This underscores the basic tension between noncharismatic and charismatic evangelicals.

In contrast to this wary stance, charismatics unitedly rejoice over all renewal movements currently stirring within mainline Protestant churches and within Catholicism (with 30 million charismatic Catholics). They find that it is precisely those evangelicals who have not separated from mainline churches who join them in praying and working for renewal. They call attention to the

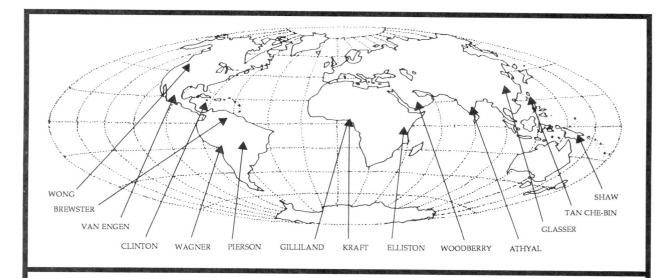

WONG
BREWSTER
VAN ENGEN
CLINTON   WAGNER   PIERSON   GILLILAND   KRAFT   ELLISTON   WOODBERRY   ATHYAL

SHAW
TAN CHE-BIN
GLASSER

hard statistics that convince them that one of God's great surprises in our day is what God is doing in virtually all the major traditions in the Christian movement. The WCC today is not promoting the secularism that characterized its Fourth Assembly at Uppsala (1968). And the Apostolic Exhortation of Pope Paul VI, "Evangelization in the Modern World" (*Evangelii Nuntiandi*, 1974), represents a very biblical and extensive (23,000 words) delineation of the missionary task (apart from a brief statement on Mary).

At the same time charismatic leaders are not unaware of their own weaknesses. Their proof-text approach to the Bible leads them to become almost too preoccupied with "signs and wonders" and the demonic, while remaining largely indifferent to a growing concern of traditional ecumenicals—that mission involves social responsibility and the obligation to be signs of the coming kingdom of God, reflecting God's justice, reconciling love, and hostility to all that provokes discrimination and poverty. Each

> **The history of evangelicals is more replete with evidence of their penchant for separating from one another than for furthering their mutual enrichment.**

evangelical group desperately needs to be balanced by the others. But the history of evangelicals is more replete with evidence of their penchant for separating from one another than for furthering their mutual enrichment.

A hopeful countersign occurred in September 1988 when a group of Christian delegates from twenty-one countries gathered at Stuttgart, West Germany, for a week-long working conference convened by the LCWE European Committee. Their objective was to take the full measure of what has been happening in Europe since 1974 and to discuss what they should do in anticipation of Lausanne II. Whereas they rejoiced in the unprecedented growth of the church in Africa, Latin America and Asia, they were burdened at the slow growth of vital Christianity in both Eastern and Western Europe. As I pondered the thrust of the Bible studies that engaged their hearts and minds, it was not difficult to catch the depth of their commitment to Christ. To read the papers they presented on the tragedy of Europe's mainline churches—so largely unaware that evangelism is their necessary task and so ineffective in challenging the secularization process that relentlessly increases the average European's doubt that God exists—was to enter into their painful concern for European church renewal. The gospel is so poorly understood and the call to conversion almost never issued.

All agreed that the spiritual paralysis within the churches is the greatest obstacle to the evangelization of Europe's spiritually hungry millions. Furthermore, the "free churches" are inhibited in Lutheran/Reformed/Catholic Europe by the attitude of the state churches toward them. And non-European mission agencies have been largely ineffective because of their lack of integrating contact with Europe's evangelicals. The "Stuttgart Call" issued at the end of this gathering included the following plea:

Come over and help us! We Christians in Europe confess that we need to learn from the churches in Africa, Asia, and the Americas in their unselfconscious, winsome ways of sharing the abundant life of Christ. So we invite the church worldwide to *work with us in partnership* for the re-evangelization of our continent and the evangelization of the areas and peoples in our countries which are still unreached.

Before the delegates parted, they committed themselves to an "ongoing cooperation" beyond Lausanne II. They plan to meet again in 1992.

Will the Riffraff Enter the WCC?

The WCC's Commission on World Mission and Evangelism (CWME) convened a consultation on evangelism in Stuttgart, West Germany, in 1987, and significantly clarified its 1982 document on "Mission and Evangelism: An Ecumenical Affirmation." This earlier document was enthusiastically received by some evangelicals (i.e., by those who read it) because of its major emphasis that "Christians owe the message of God's salvation in Jesus Christ to every person and to every people" (paragraph 41). Those who met at Stuttgart included almost a score of evangelicals from churches not related to the WCC, plus an equal number of conciliar evangelicals. Together they generated materials for the theological preparation of the CWME's World Mission Conference at San Antonio, Texas, just six weeks before Lausanne II. The theme of this gathering will be "Your Will Be Done: Mission in Christ's Way."

The interaction at Stuttgart was so positive that it was suggested that CWME, WEF, and LCWE should consider appointing a joint committee to lift up models of evangelism that all could agree were authentic and adequate representations of the gospel. Inasmuch as Lausanne II is concerned to motivate the whole church to take the whole gospel to the whole world, its leaders can hardly fail to respond to this suggestion.

Emilio Castro, the general secretary of the WCC, has expressed his desire to encourage all attempts to bring Christians together for the sake of the mission and renewal of the church. The January 1988 issue of the *Ecumenical Review*, edited by Castro, included an excellent essay by Donald H. Dayton. Its cryptic title, "Yet Another Layer of the Onion," is amplified with the subtitle: "Or Opening the Ecumenical Door to Let the Riffraff In." In masterful fashion Dayton shows how inadequately representative the WCC actually is of the worldwide Christian movement. Its ecclesiastical "mainstream" represents barely half of all Protestants. Castro commends this lengthy article because he wants readers to be aware of "the historiographical and theological significance of the Holiness, Pentecostal and Keswick movements and the churches which trace their origin to them"—in short, the nonconciliar evangelicals.

Further, Castro endorses Dayton's view that evangelicals represent a layer of Christian truth and commitment without which the ecumenical movement remains incomplete. Then Castro adds: "[This] is an issue that needs to be faced, not least because of the historical commitment of these movements to what today are recognized as ecumenical concerns" (1988, p. 3). But will WEF and its member churches of noncharismatic evangelicals respond to this challenge? Or will they oppose CWME's World Conference ("Mission in Christ's Way") while supporting LCWE's International Congress ("Proclaim Christ Until He Comes")? In

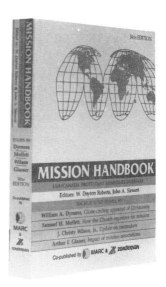

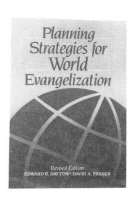

matters of this sort nonconciliar evangelicals and charismatics seriously disagree, but not primarily for biblical reasons.

A.D. 2000 and Beyond

One cannot mention the evangelical need for networking without calling attention to their growing fascination with the year A.D. 2000. The recent multiplication of plans by evangelicals to complete the evangelization of all unreached peoples by then has stimulated some digging into history. In fact, a book by David Barrett and James Reapsome was published late in 1988 entitled *Seven Hundred Plans to Evangelize the World*. This staggering compilation bears eloquent witness to evangelicalism's strengths and its weaknesses. More than 780 global plans, originating in seventy-one separate countries, have emerged since Pentecost, when the New Testament church began. Over 400 plans expired in less than five years, but about 250 are alive today. Among them "over 50 are multimillion-dollar megaplans, each involving colossal resources of personnel, finance, and logistics. And over half of them have announced the year 2000 as their deadline" (Bush, 1988, p. 24). This is mind-boggling!

What mystifies the average evangelical confronted by all this dynamism, global vision, and monumental expense is how to relate these programs to the painful fact that "an average of 53,000 people leave the Christian church from one Sunday to the next in Europe and North America" (Bosch, 1987, p. 13). That evangelical hears Lesslie Newbigin raise the question whether or not the West can really be converted to Jesus Christ. When our evangelical learns that seventy-seven countries are currently closed to traditional evangelistic activity and that few of these megaplans for world evangelization are in touch with one another, despite attempts to bring their leaders together, he or she begins to wonder whether American corporate triumphalism is not taking over the evangelical empire.

Even so, one should neither downplay nor underestimate the desire of Christians to obey their Lord's last command. Recently, over 4,000 Indonesian evangelical leaders met and after several days of earnest prayer and prolonged discussion pledged themselves to share the gospel with every person in their country by the year 2000 and also train at least 5,000 to serve in other countries as evangelists and church planters. Furthermore, they convened this gathering with very little financial assistance from abroad.

But Questions Linger

What should we say to all this? Perhaps at this point we should draw back from the fascination of "A.D. 2000 and beyond" and reflect on some of the more tangible foci of the current evangelical discussions as leaders peer into the future and make global plans. These foci have been detailed by Ralph Winter (1985), David Hesselgrave (1987), Howard Snyder and Daniel Runyon (1987), and Luis Bush (1988), among others. One immediately notices no reference to global economic realities. Apparently, it would be a sign of unbelief to factor into these bold plans such distracting issues as the growing poverty and unrelieved indebtedness of the nations of the two-thirds world, and the U.S. shift in the past decade from a lender to a debtor nation. In contrast, a naive assumption is present and not challenged: the world's economy will increasingly become more buoyant. Whereas "church incomes by the year 2000 will increase to no more than 80 billion

dollars" it is expected that "para-church and institutional income will jump to a whopping 120 billion!" (Hesselgrave, 1988a, p. 12).

Furthermore, despite the changes rapidly taking place throughout the world, another tacit assumption is that the mission society and missionary role developed in the eighteenth century will prevail into the twenty-first century. Both will remain central—so it is thought—to efforts to evangelize the nations. All that is needed, apparently, is more missionaries (one report calls for 100,000 of them) and more mission agencies of the nineteenth-century pattern.

Local churches will doubtless be recognized *en courant*, but they will not direct "the final push." This assumed dichotomy is to be deplored, for churches attain maturity only through themselves attaining centrality in the task of evangelizing their own peoples and reaching out beyond their own cultural frontiers to extend the good news of the kingdom. Of course, we believe that the work of Jesus Christ in the midst of Christ's people will continue. But evangelicals have no grounds for assuming that the mission agencies of today will automatically be the strategic vehicles God will be using as the church enters its third millennium.

We are also told that the Christian church has come alive powerfully in China over the past ten years or so, and it is suggested that this resurgence of Chinese Christianity is likely to impact world Christianity in a variety of ways. The assumption is that the impact will be positive and challenging. Granted, the estimates of the number of Christians in the People's Republic today range between 30 and 50 million. Those of us who served as missionaries there prior to the Maoist revolution cannot but rejoice over this phenomenal explosion of Christians.

But why is this picture painted only in glowing colors? What of the darker side? This tremendous Christward movement is almost entirely a peasant phenomenon. It has barely touched the cities, much less the educated Chinese. Some Chinese Christian scholars say that its current impact on the nation is almost negligible. Those who have interviewed many non-Christian Chinese graduate students currently in the West find them to be totally unaware of this peasant movement. Furthermore, China's rural house-church believers are largely untaught and poorly led. I've heard responsible Chinese Christian scholars say that this movement is perilously close to becoming something not unlike Africa's independent churches—uneven mixtures of biblical faith and animistic folk religion.

This drift can be halted and reversed only by greatly adjusting the flow of radio broadcasts to their leaders (who, we know, are listening). And special attention must be given to penetrating the unreached world of the Chinese intelligentsia. It is tragic that Kairos Broadcasting Service—the largest producer of programs for broadcast to both rural and urban segments of Chinese society via Far East Broadcasting Co. and Trans World Radio—is currently struggling to survive. Initially, the Kairos Broadcasting Service (KBS) was launched by Norwegian and Finnish evangelical groups and greatly helped by German and American Lutherans. Through the Lutheran World Federation verbal approval was gained from the Three-Self Patriotic Movement. More recently this approval was withdrawn, and now some of the major supporting churches are being pressured to draw back and terminate their relationship with KBS. It would be a tragedy if this specially designed broadcasting were to cease.

We might also mention the task of evangelizing the Muslim world. Can this be accomplished by A.D. 2000? I would not presume to say, but I count as my friends all who proclaim the gospel to this massive segment of the human race especially because Muslims are turning to Christ today. In some countries significant breakthroughs are taking place, especially where Islam's rootage in society is intertwined with indigenous animism and where what can only be termed Folk Islam has been the result. In Bangladesh, Indonesia, and Burkina Faso, local converts when carefully trained have been significantly involved in leading these movements, assisted in some places by expatriate missionaries. One should also note that due to the recently terminated eight-year war between Iraq and Iran as well as the Soviet invasion of Afghanistan, thousands upon thousands of Muslims have been killed or wounded, millions have been displaced, and untold numbers have been caught up in this anguish. In their suffering and need, many a Muslim has turned to Jesus, the Prophet Who Heals, and has cried out for his compassion. As a result, field reports often speak of Muslims coming to faith in Christ and seeking to contact the Christian community.

However, these reports all too often lament the lack of spiritual vitality and evangelistic concern that characterize many churches throughout the Middle East. The strategic task is to pray for their renewal. Although radio broadcasting and correspondence courses are causing many Muslims to reflect on the gospel, these churches are crucial to the evangelization of the Muslim world. Whereas missionaries are still welcome, not only from the West, but from Asia, Latin America, and Africa, they should not function apart from close association with these churches.

I bring this study to an abrupt end. The creativity of the Holy Spirit will continue to match the political, economic, and sociological changes taking place in the world. New mission structures and support patterns will emerge, but they will no longer be Western-dominated. Missionaries from the two-thirds world will increasingly occupy the center of the stage. Indeed, the internationalization of the missionary movement is "the great new fact of our time." Evangelicals show every evidence of growing in numbers and maturity as we approach A.D. 2000. But their response to the challenges of the days ahead means that tomorrow's missionary obedience will hardly resemble what we see around us today.

References

Barrett, David B., and James W. Reapsome. 1988. *Seven Hundred Plans to Evangelize the World: The Rise of a Global Evangelization Movement.* Birmingham, Ala.: New Hope.

Bosch, David J. 1987. "Vision for Mission." *International Review of Mission.* Vol. 76, no. 301, pp. 8–15.

Brunner, Emil. 1946. *Revelation and Reason: The Christian Doctrine of Faith and Reason.* Philadelphia: Westminster Press.

Bush, Luis. 1988. "Eight Principles for World Evangelization by the Year 2000." *World Evangelization.* Vol. 15, no. 52, pp. 22–24.

Castro, Emilio. 1988. "Editorial." *Ecumenical Review.* Vol. 39, no. 1, pp. 1–3.

Dayton, Donald H. 1988. "Yet Another Layer of the Onion." *Ecumenical Review.* Vol. 39, no. 1, pp. 87–110.

Hesselgrave, David J. 1987. "Major Trends and Issues in World Missions Today." *Evangelical Missions Quarterly.* Vol. 23, no. 3, pp. 298–305.

———1988a. "Ten Major Trends in World Missions." *World Evangelization.* Vol. 15, no. 52, pp. 12–14.

———1988b. *Today's Choices for Tomorrow's Mission: An Evangelical Perspective on Trends and Issues.* Grand Rapids: Zondervan.

Snyder, Howard A., and Daniel V. Runyon. 1986. *Foresight: Ten Major Trends That Will Dramatically Affect the Future of Christians and the Church.* Nashville, Tenn.: Thomas Nelson.

———1987. "Ten Major Trends Facing the Church." *International Bulletin of Missionary Research.* Vol. 11, no. 2, pp. 67–70.

Theological News [publication of World Evangelical Fellowship]. 1988. Report of Theodore Williams, W.E.F. president. Vol. 20, no. 2, pp. 2–3.

Warren, M.A.C. 1962. *The Sevenfold Secret.* London: S.P.C.K.

Webber, Robert E., and Donald Bloesch. 1978. *The Orthodox Evangelicals: Who They Are and What They Are Saying.* Nashville, Tenn.: Thomas Nelson.

Winter, Ralph D. 1987. "What Is World Evangelization and Is It Possible to Achieve?" *Mission Frontiers.* Vol. 9, no. 7, p. 5.

The Church as Servant of the Coming Kingdom

Michael Amaladoss, S.J.

Every Christian is on mission, called to witness, in word and deed, to the gift of God that he or she has received. But the situation of the world in which we are will condition the type of witness that we are called to render. Therefore, before we go on to reflect on the tasks of mission in the 1990s, it will be good to consider briefly the factors of today's world that are relevant to such a reflection.

Contemporary Challenges

The age of mission that took Christianity to Asia, Africa, and Latin America coincided with the colonial period. While the interests of the colonialists and the missionaries did not always coincide, the missionaries certainly profited by the logistics provided by the colonial structures. We are now living in a largely postcolonial situation, at least politically. With political freedom, there is a resurgence of religions and cultures everywhere, providing new national identities, sometimes marginalizing the churches as "foreign" elements.

Our view of evangelization has been widening in two directions. We no longer think of mission as only the proclamation of a message that is assented to in faith. Today we also think of a faith that does justice. We think of faith as a commitment that calls to action for the integral liberation of the human being, for salvation is not merely for the "soul," but for the whole human person (Lk. 4:16–21). Second, there has been a growing appreciation both of other religions as having a positive role in the divine plan of salvation, and of the freedom of each person's conscience even in matters of religion, so that interreligious dia-

Michael Amaladoss, a Jesuit from Tamil Nadu, South India, is one of the Assistants to the Superior General of the Society of Jesus, Rome. Previously he was a professor at Vidyajyoti, Institute of Religious Studies, Delhi, and editor of Vidyajyoti, *a journal of theological reflection published in Delhi.*

logue has become an integral dimension of evangelization. The very use of the word "evangelization" in place of "mission" is indicative of this difference in perspective.

Mission is no longer considered as the work of missionaries who leave their country to proclaim the gospel in strange lands. Mission has its origin in the Trinity, with the Son and the Spirit being sent into the world. The *whole church*, as the servant of this plan of God, *is in mission.* Moreover, the church seems to be in a mission situation everywhere in the world—in the six continents. In the former mission countries, while the church as an institution may have been founded everywhere at least in a small way, it has not really become a local church, transforming the local cultures in the power of the Spirit. The Christian countries, because of a wave of secularization, have become post-Christian, so that they are in need of a second evangelization.

It is to this world that we are sent. Looking at mission from these perspectives, I would like to point to just five areas that demand our serious attention in the coming decade.

Evangelization as Liberation

The most striking thing about our world today is the poverty of the majority of humanity. Christ came with the good news to these poor people. Missionaries have always been aware of this dimension in their work. Hospitals and orphanages, schools and developmental projects have always borne witness to Christian charity all over the world. But today we are realizing that the poor are not merely poor, but are made poor by unjust economic and political structures. A privatized, otherworldly religion may have become an alienating force. The media and other cultural forces may have created a spirit of dependence and resignation among the poor. The rich too become prisoners of structures that often they have not created but inherited. The word of liberation to the poor is at the same time a word of condemnation and prophetic challenge to the rich and the powerful. The division between the rich and the poor is not merely a problem among the nations, but also within each nation. A difference in ideologies—liberal capitalism or state socialism—does not really make any difference as far as the oppressive structures are concerned.

Proclaiming the gospel in this situation is to proclaim liberation—not merely economic and political, but also cultural and religious. These dimensions are interlinked. This would mean today conscientizing the people and helping them to organize themselves to struggle for their own liberation—for the kingdom of peace, freedom, fellowship, and justice that God has promised for all peoples. Evangelization that takes such an integral approach cannot but have a *political dimension.* The church and the missionaries will have to confront prophetically the powers that be. The church-institution may not become a political party. But the Christians, who are also in mission, can neither stand apart from politics nor bracket their faith convictions from political action. One can very well imagine groups of people witnessing to the gospel in the first world while fighting for justice for the poor in the third world. After all the precautions have been taken—avoiding violence, and so forth—liberation becomes an integral dimension of evangelization.

A Holistic View of Mission

In this activity of promoting justice and peace we may find in other religions allies rather than enemies as the event of religious leaders praying together for peace in Assisi, in October 1986, made evident. A deeper reflection on this event will show that while we have to be loyal to the revelation that we have received from God in Jesus Christ and to the mission to share it with all peoples in word and deed, we have also to be respectful not only of the freedom of the others, both as persons and as groups, to seek God sincerely in the best way known to them, but also of the freedom of God who is communicating to humankind in ways known and unknown to us. Such respect will be manifested as dialogue with believers of other religions.

Interreligious dialogue supposes the acceptance of the basic unity of God's plan in creation and redemption that embraces all peoples (1 Tim. 2:4; Rom. 2:6–11). Within this universal plan of God we have to articulate the particular mission of Jesus and of the church in leading actively this divine plan to its final consummation. One of the burning questions, old but ever new, of the next decade will be how do we articulate the universality of God's action in the world and the particularity of God's intervention in Jesus. The relationship between these two moments in the history of salvation may be seen in different ways. Some will see these two moments as discontinuous. If the first moment is seen as creation, then the two moments will be opposed as natural and supernatural. If one stresses, rather, the fall in the beginning, then one will oppose the two moments as sinful and salvific. One will then be eloquent on the scandal of particularity. Others will see them as two dialectical moments of a single plan of God. The Jesus event is of course unique, with universal significance and with a decisive impact on the course of history. But this mission is in continuity with the mission of the word through whom God made all things (see John 1:3). The mission of Jesus cannot be fully understood unless it is set back in the context of the history of all God's peoples. In Jesus we have an assurance of a new world. But this new world will have to be realized now and in the future. We have to build it up. It is God's gift, but also our task. The task of mission is precisely to make present the inspiration and power of Jesus and the Spirit in the movement of history toward its fulfillment.

Dialogue and Witness

Proclamation or witness that respects the freedom both of the individual and of God cannot but be dialogical. Correspondingly the aim of dialogue is not merely to promote mutual knowledge and understanding, but also to witness to one's deepest faith convictions and thus provide a challenge to mutual growth toward the common end, namely, God. Such dialogue is neither syncretistic nor relativistic. It does not suppose that all religions are the same or that everything is true. But it demands a respect that discerns God's presence and action wherever it is found and a humility that does not have any exclusive claim to God's truth and love. No one today holds the axiom "There is no salvation outside the church." One also notices a growing openness not only to the great religions, but also to the cosmic (popular) religions and to the new religious movements.

It is in such a holistic perspective of the plan of God for the world that we have to spell out what it really means to be a disciple of Christ, what is the specific identity of the church and its mission in the world, what is the dynamism that moves world history in hope, in the context of the creative freedoms both of God and of the people. Such a holistic viewpoint will transcend the dispute that one reads about in missiological literature between Chris-

tocentrism and Theocentrism by contemplating the *Trinity*, where there is neither center nor periphery, so that one does not have to defend Christ by opposing Christ to the Father and Spirit. The Trinity communicates is own dynamism of love and life to the mission that will gather up into a unity the whole universe that God may be all in all (1 Cor. 15:28; cf. Eph. 1:3–14; Rom. 8:19–25).

A Humble Witness

A mission that is respectful of this trinitarian mystery will be humble. It is one thing to be aware of the privilege of having had an experience of God's self-manifestation and to bear witness to it boldly and clearly. It is another thing to pretend to be an exclusive messenger of God and not be attentive to God's continuing action in the world. One thinks of how Peter would have felt at the house of Cornelius at Joppa (Acts 10). Another reason for humility is the respect that one should have for the freedom of the other person. What is important is the relationship between God and this other—and I am only a humble facilitator of this relationship.

In Jesus we have an assurance of a new world.

With the end of the colonial era, missions no longer have the backing of the political power. One wonders whether the economic backing that many missions have even today is an unmixed blessing. In India, for example, the church-institution has the image of unlimited resources compared to the Christian community, which is largely poor. While much of this money goes to the poor through charitable institutions, schools, and the like, the church does project a "foreign" image. This could be one reason why its witness is not taken as seriously as it would like. The example of China in recent years shows that poverty and even persecution are not obstacles to mission, but may be advantages. They make it credible and authentic. That was the way of Christ, who came not in power but in humility, and was obedient even unto death (Phil. 2:6–11). Once we see the gospel not only as a message to be assented to but as a call to commitment and change of life and structures, then the credibility of our witness is also affected by the behavior of the people identified as Christian, both in the colonial era and in modern times. Besides, the rapidity with which these countries seem to have become dechristianized in recent years might raise questions in the mind of the people about the way the Christians have been able to face the challenges of the modern world.

A Spiritual Humanism

These challenges of the modern world will, I think, dominate the agenda of mission in the 1990s. Science, while it helps us to discover the secrets of nature, seems to encourage an empirical and positivist spirit that promotes experiment and verification as the only criterion of truth, thus denying transcendence. Technology that helps us to make use of scientific knowledge to control nature and to produce goods falls a prey to consumerism. When empiricism and consumerism are uncontrolled by human and spiritual values we have all the evils of modern society. Science and technology could be used for the benefit of all. But they, rather, serve the pursuit of pleasure and the search for power and domination. The temptations of plenty are not new. But the speed and facility of modern communications and the power of technology have made life a mad rush for success so that families, relationships, human attitudes, attention to the common good, and concern for ultimate values have all broken down.

What is the challenge of the good news to this situation? One should avoid the temptation to blame science and technology, or industrialization, for all these ills. They are tools in our hands. We have been misusing them for our own personal and collective selfish ends. The gospel, in collaboration with other religions, can certainly promote a spiritual humanism. It is a humanism insofar as it affirms the priority of human values like love, freedom, fellowship, and peace over inhuman ones like the pursuit of power and pleasure, exploitation, selfishness, the subordination of the human to the machine, and the subjugation of the common good to market forces. It is spiritual insofar as such a humanism will be authentic only when it is rooted in God, in the meaning of life and the plan of salvation God has for each one and for humanity.

It is more difficult to inculturate a church that is already established than to let a new local church emerge.

Collaboration in Mission

We spoke above about mission being a reality in six continents. The church is a small community everywhere in mission. Even in the so-called Christian countries the true believers are in a minority. It is in this new context that we should rethink the traditional idea of "foreign" missions. Today we would rather say that mission anywhere is primarily the responsibility of the *local church*. But every local church, being in communion with all the other local churches, is also responsible for universal mission. Therefore it must be open to go out and help, when there is need, or just as a symbol of this communion—the catholicity of the church.

This means first of all that in every place the church has to be really local. The missionary efforts of the recent centuries may have succeeded in planting the church-institution everywhere. But it has not really favored the emergence of the local church, which is the incarnation of the gospel in a particular people, culture, and reality. One speaks very much about *inculturation* today. But that is a task that is still before us. It is more difficult to inculturate a church that is already established than to let a new local church emerge. But we do not have a choice in the matter. The church has to become local, not only because otherwise the Christians themselves will feel alienated from the reality of their lives, but also in order precisely to be on effective mission in the local situation. Otherwise the church will be proclaiming a disembodied message. It has to confront the realities of the local situation and show concretely in life and action the relevance of the gospel. Besides, in a postcolonial situation, with the growing self-affirmation of many countries, only the local church can be sensitive and responsible for an authentic and effective proclamation of the gospel in many difficult situations.

If mission is primarily the responsibility of the local church, then cross-cultural mission is at the service of the local church. This service is not merely a help in need but also a witness to a different cultural appropriation of the gospel so that a living dialogue between these various appropriations may lead to growing convergence and communion among the churches through mutual enrichment. From this point of view one should think in terms of cross-cultural mission not only from the North to the South and from the West to the East, but also from the South to the North and from the East to the West.

In a divided world searching for peace and justice, the task of mission is not only to build up countercultural communities as a foretaste of the kingdom, but also to animate peoples' movements that will re-create the world in the power of the Spirit (see Rev. 21:1–8).

Challenges and Hindrances to the Unfinished Task

Johannes Verkuyl

I was born in the first decade of this century, two years before the Edinburgh World Missionary Conference of 1910, where it was affirmed that every generation has the obligation to preach the gospel in word and deed to its contemporaries.

Now we are approaching the last decade of the twentieth century. In this "century of catastrophes" I have seen all the suffering and wickedness of which Jesus spoke in Matthew 24 and Mark 13, but I have also seen something of the positive promise in those same chapters: "This gospel of the kingdom will be preached throughout the whole world, as a testimony to all nations" (Matt. 24:14). When I think about the harvest of the storms in this century in regard to that promise, I would mention three items about which a consensus developed in the earlier decades of this century, not only in the official world mission conferences but also in local and national settings all over the world.

1. The goal of mission is the kingdom of God, and the communication of the gospel of the kingdom has four dimensions: proclamation, diakonia, fellowship, and participation in the struggle against all kinds of injustices and for righteousness and peace.

2. The task should be fulfilled in cooperation among churches in all six continents; communication of the gospel means a task *in, from,* and *to* all six continents.

3. We need each other not only in theological developments, but also in the proclamation of the gospel of the kingdom, in the diaconate, in the building of "koinonia," and in the struggle against injustices and for righteousness and shalom. We cannot

Johannes Verkuyl is Emeritus Professor of Missiology and Evangelism, Faculty of Theology, Free University of Amsterdam. His book Contemporary Missiology *(Eerdmans, 1978) is widely used as a textbook.*

say to each other, "I do not need you." "For just as the body is one and has many members, and all the members of the body, though many, are one body, so it is with Christ" (1 Cor. 12:12).

As we enter the last decade of this century, we confess that the task of world mission is unfinished and our common calling is to carry on with this task. When we consider the unfinished task we see challenges and hindrances to which we should give attention.

The Unreached

The gospel of the kingdom should be preached from decade to decade, from culture to culture, from continent to continent. In every nation there are thousands and even millions of people who have not been reached with the gospel. I never understand why "ecumenicals" and "evangelicals" do not cooperate more to reach the unreached. There are many consultations—national, regional, continental, worldwide—among churches. But in ecumenical circles these consultations concentrate mostly within the ecclesiastical network to strengthen internal church structures. Why don't we ask each other: What can we do to assist each other to reach the unreached in our countries?

Statisticians such as David B. Barrett and his associates provide us with ample material about the unreached in all countries of the world. Why don't we make better use of that material and why is it so often the case that "evangelicals" pay attention to the unreached while "ecumenicals" make snide remarks about the effort? I would urge that both sides should help each other to strengthen the structures of the churches and at the same time pay attention to the unreached. Strengthening the structures of the churches should be strengthening the structures of the *missionary congregation* to reach the unreached. I agree with Bishop Lesslie Newbigin that the "enduring validity of crosscultural mission" is necessary in all directions. This is not the time to preach again the "gospel of the moratorium" as was done at the Bangkok Conference in 1972–73. This is the time for a new initiative in cooperation to reach those who have not yet heard the gospel.

> ## What is the crisis? It is the tendency to play down the centrality, the decisiveness of the person and work of Jesus Christ.

The Crisis in Interfaith Dialogue

Everyone who has followed the discussions and developments in interfaith dialogue in recent years should be aware that there is a crisis in interfaith dialogue.

The *International Review of Mission* of July 1988, with the theme "Tambaram Revisited," demonstrates this crisis most clearly. The debate between Wilfred Cantwell Smith and Lesslie Newbigin at the Tambaram anniversary celebration in 1988 illustrates the crisis, but the symptoms were evident throughout the consultation, as they are evident in many parts of the world. Harvey

Cox, who has not only a remarkable feeling for what is in the air but also a charisma to call a spade a spade, has written about the crisis in interfaith dialogue.[1] I think there are many reasons to speak of a crisis, and it is better to admit it than to hide it with sophisticated words.

What is the crisis? It is the tendency to play down the centrality, the decisiveness of the person and work of Jesus Christ, in interfaith dialogue, and to move from the Christocentric and trinitarian basis of the World Council of Churches (WCC) to a so-called theocentric point of view. In one of the last letters I received from Dr. W. A. Visser 't Hooft before his death, he wrote that in his long lifetime, again and again he saw the rise of a wave of theological relativism, and that he saw such a wave coming again. He expressed the hope that the WCC would stand firm on its theological basis in the midst of this new wave of relativism.

There is indeed a new drift now toward religious universalism and theological relativism, especially in the dialogue program, that will pose more and more serious questions not only about the credibility of the WCC, but even about its survival. The San Antonio World Mission Conference should help us in this impasse between mission and dialogue.

It is my conviction that the nature of dialogue should be that of *trialogue*, as was properly formulated and expressed at the World Mission Conference in Mexico City in 1963: "Whatever the circumstances may be, our intention in every human dialogue should be to be involved in the dialogue of God with men, and to move our partner and ourself to listen to what God in Christ reveals to us, and to answer Him."[2]

We not only need dialogue for mutual understanding and cooperation, but we also need missionary dialogues that involve the *trialogue* between God and ourselves with people of other faiths. The San Antonio Mission Conference must address the impasse and crisis in interfaith dialogue. It must also clarify the relation between the Commission on World Mission and Evangelism (CWME), and the subunit on Dialogue in such a way that the WCC does not speak from both sides of its mouth, but speaks on the basis of our common trinitarian confession of faith.

The Issue of Religious Liberty

After World War II the Commission on International Affairs of the WCC-in-process-of-formation was deeply involved in the formulation of the Declaration on Human Rights of the United Nations. Under the able leadership of O. Frederick Nolde this commission was also deeply involved in the struggle to integrate religious liberty in the constitutions of the emerging and independent states in Asia and Africa. I saw Nolde at work in Asia in those crucial times. There was reason for optimism in regard to the implementation of this fundamental right in practice.

Afterward it was stressed—and rightly so—that we should not forget the interrelation between religious liberty and social, economic, and cultural-ecological justice. But nowadays we realize that contemporary history cannot be compared with a daybreak in this field. In many parts of the world we see a cloud coming up from the side of totalitarian political systems and "religious" states, which try to maintain control over their citizens with oppressive state power.

There is an unbelievable threat to human rights in general and religious liberty in particular. Theo van Boven, the former director of the Human Rights Commission of the United Nations, wrote recently: "Fundamentalist movements in religion are a threat and a menace to the universality of human rights in general and for religious liberty especially."

This topic should have high priority on the agenda of the San Antonio Mission Conference as a topic for serious discussion. The proclamation of the gospel of the kingdom does not depend on the implementation of human rights, but this proclamation should nonetheless be protected by law. This issue had high priority immediately after World War II, and it is time to give it careful attention again.

Participation of the Churches in the Western World in the Unfinished Task of World Mission

More and more there is a tendency to write off the participation of churches in the Western world in the unfinished task of world mission. At the World Missionary Conference in Edinburgh and during the time of the Student Volunteer Movement in the beginning of this century, there was a kind of Western triumphalism. Now there is a polycentrism in the fulfillment of world mission. The churches in the Western world are deeply thankful for this miracle and they are also humbled by God's judgment

> More and more there is a tendency to write off the participation of churches in the Western world in the unfinished task of world mission.

over their triumphalism. But now we see this tendency among some influential Westerners to write off the Western churches in terms of any further role in the task of world evangelization.

I do not underrate the "cancer of the soul" in the Western world, and the moral and spiritual decline in the Western part of the "global village." I believe that Alan Bloom is right when he writes about the loss of orientation and the loss of living belief in the Western world. The analysis of Lesslie Newbigin in his *Foolishness to the Greeks* is full of shameful truth. Movements like "New Age" are a sign that thousands in the Western world seek an answer to the deepest questions of human life but do not seek the answers anymore in the message of the Christian tradition and the churches. Sometimes Western critics of the Western missions remind me of the flagellants of the Middle Ages in Europe, with the difference that the flagellants of the twelfth and thirteenth centuries flagellated themselves; whereas the modern Western flagellants flog the old missionary personnel and pray: "God, we thank Thee that we are not like those old missionaries." Then they go away and do nothing.

I place my hope on a younger generation of women and men in the Western world who are humble enough to assist their Asian, African, and Latin American colleagues, and I hope that friends from other continents will help us in the West to assist the Christian minority in the toughest mission field of the world: the North Atlantic world. But we should not be desperate or discouraged.

Lamin Sanneh from the Gambia, who is the new professor of mission and world Christianity at Yale Divinity School, has written about the "guilt-complex of western missionaries."[3] He encourages us to do our homework in our own nations, and he encourages the younger generation to participate in world mission in new ways.

Not long before his death, Stephen Neill gave an analysis about the self-criticism in Western churches, and he discussed the many reasons for that self-criticism and for penitence.[4] Self-criticism of Western missions is necessary but it should not lead to defeat and paralysis. Rather, it should foster renewal and new initiatives in mission for our situation today.

Rapprochement between Evangelicals and Ecumenicals Is Needed for the Unfinished Task of World Mission

One of the most noteworthy developments in the 1980s was the document "Mission and Evangelism: An Ecumenical Affirmation," approved by the WCC Central Committee in July 1982. This "ecumenical affirmation" was the result of close cooperation between ecumenicals and evangelicals, and it has been widely used as a study guide for congregations. It is my conviction that every evangelical (in the New Testament sense of that word) should be an ecumenical, and every ecumenical (in the biblical sense and also in the sense in which it was used by the pioneers of the ecumenical movement) should be an evangelical.

Today, however the distance between evangelicals and ecumenicals is growing wider, and we are faced with the threat of polarization between these two traditions. What we need in the 1990s is not polarization but rapprochement. It is time to get serious about this problem and to take deliberate steps at bridge-building.

At a time when the Vatican is moving more and more in the direction of a new "counter-reformation," it is ironic that many mainline ecumenical Protestant churches cooperate more closely

---

> It is my conviction that every evangelical should be an ecumenical, and every ecumenical should be an evangelical.

---

with the Vatican than with Protestant evangelicals. We should be grateful for the many contacts between the WCC and the Roman Catholic Church during and after Vatican Council II, but it is likely that the official trend in the Vatican in the 1990s will continue more in the direction of counter-reformation than co-reformation. We should certainly continue official contacts with the Vatican, but on the national, regional, and continental levels we should strengthen our relations with those groups within the Roman Catholic Church that, in spite of heavy pressure from the Vatican, are still moving in the direction of a co-reformation.

Mission in the 1990s needs Christians and churches that work in the spirit of the document "Mission and Evangelism: An Ecumenical Affirmation." Our task now is to put flesh on the spirit of that document, in our words and deeds.

The Lord's Promise

Jesus promised to be with us "all the days," to the end of time (Matt. 28:20). This promise is related to the unfinished task of world mission. Therefore we must always ask: Which day is it today? What is the importance of this decade for the Christian world mission?

If we should miss or dismiss the promise and the presence of the crucified and risen Lord in the continuation of missionary work, our task would be a lost cause, a meaningless enterprise. We would make concessions to the professional pessimists who think it is their task to spread alarm and defeatism. But within the light of the Lord's promise and presence, the continuation of the church's mission in the last decade of this century will not be a lost cause or a meaningless enterprise, since we know that in the Lord our labor cannot be in vain.

Notes

1. Harvey Cox, "Many Mansions or One Way? The Crisis in Interfaith Dialogue," *Christian Century*, August 17–24, 1988, pp. 731–35.
2. Ronald K. Orchard, ed., *Witness in Six Continents: Records of the Meeting of the Commission on World Mission and Evangelism of the World Council of Churches Held in Mexico City, December 8th to 9th, 1963* (London: Edinburgh House Press, 1964), p. 147.
3. Lamin Sanneh, "Christian Missions and the Western Guilt Complex," *Christian Century*, April 8, 1987, pp. 330–34.
4. Stephen Neill, *Salvation Tomorrow* (Nashville, Tenn.: Abingdon, 1976), pp. 18ff.

Mission Tomorrow: Nothing Will Be Easy

Anna Marie Aagaard

Europe and Mission

Recently a Danish sculptor told some traveling reporters about his life and times. From his present base in northern Italy he reminisced about years spent in India with stonemasons in search of the secrets of their craft. The sculptor went on to tell about his homecoming to Europe and the culture shock he was going through. He did not elaborate on taxes, politics, or affluency, but went straight to the issue of religious traditions and their impact on cultures.

Much was commonplace in his observations, but a couple of sentences stood out. The return to Europe and its religious symbols had made this Dane understand why Christianity was not a viable option for him, and why the cross had lost its hold on so many Europeans. From his perspective the crucifix, with the thorn-crowned head and mutilated limbs, is an apotheosis of violence—a cult symbol with long, dark shadows reaching right into the high-tech world with its violence against nature.

When the cross becomes a symbol of violence without reference to the victim and to the resurrection of the crucified Christ, the No to Christian faith becomes different from the No's that Europeans have been accustomed to during modernity's history of secularization. Churches and individual believers may not have been too successful in dealing with rationality's No to transcendence, but successive mission endeavors and a continuous theological struggle have at least found some ways to communicate the gospel as good news to secularized women and men. Mission in the 1990s in Europe will, however, encounter more and more of the No's that are not secular No's to transcendence and a religious attitude to life, but a religious affirmation of a different transcendence, an Ultimate that looks a whole lot different from

Anna Marie Aagaard is Professor of Systematic Theology, University of Aarhus, Denmark.

the God of the crucified and resurrected Christ. Many of those who dissociate themselves from Christianity, view the God of the crucified Christ as far too violent. What is affirmed may be a cosmological highest principle yielding power over destinies and shaping everyday existence; it may be a hierarchy of spirits to be sought in various ways, or a fertility goddess as a symbol of personified reproductive powers. What is new are not the variants of a spiritual, transcendent realm, but the fact that European pagans (the word is not a haughty misnomer, but is used as self-identification) want to affirm *both* a post-Christian religious attitude *and* the values, the freedoms, and the inalienable rights of European culture and legislation permeated by Christian beliefs and Christian tradition.

I am not convinced that European churches and transconfessional mission groups have the theology, and leadership (let alone the strategies) for bringing a gospel of good news in Jesus Christ to this strata of Europeans. I surmise that what mission in Europe has taken for granted, namely, some shared values as preliminary ground for preaching the gospel, will have to get on the mission agenda in the 1990s. Values, freedoms, and rights are no free-floating, ahistorical, and eternal entities. What happens to these things if they increasingly are combined with a variety of post-Christian beliefs and cut off from faith in a God whose love is manifest in justice, solidarity, care for the weak and the dying, and in the overcoming of death's destruction?

Ethics and Dialogue

My concern with words and attitudes, lifestyles and actions that will allow European pagans to encounter the Ultimate as truth and love in Jesus Christ will have to be differentiated from the future dialogue with the faithful of the world religions. Till well into the 1980s there was more "dialogue about dialogue" among Christians than actual interreligious dialogue in Western Europe. That picture is changing. And it will have to change in the 1990s. With refugees and immigrants even northern European cities are becoming "rainbow cities" in the sense that here live a growing number of people who profess variants of Hinduism, Buddhism, and Islam, and who want to keep, develop, and hand on the lifestyles, the values, and the cultures in which these religions were first inculturated.

It seems to me that interreligious dialogue at present is dominated by three approaches from the Christian side. Some argue from a hope for convergence of religious traditions; others from an inclusivist understanding of the universal Christ; and yet others argue from a distinction between a universal revelation and a particular salvation linked to the church and the profession of Christ as Lord and Savior. Whatever the stance, it presupposes the willingness of the Other to engage in a religious project with some universal claims. These divergent perspectives also impact the hope for an evolved Christianity within a "unitive pluralism."

But what will happen to interreligious dialogue if the Other refuses to be a part of such a project? What happens when organized Hinduism and Buddhism on the Indian subcontinent and in the Far East decide that religion cannot that easily become aculturated; that religion comes with the particular culture in which it was first embedded; that regions and countries with cultural roots in Hinduism and Buddhism must update their heritage and restrict (even more) the possibilities of dialogue, not to mention conversions to Christianity or visas for expatriate church personnel?

Interreligious dialogue, as we know it, may go on among "professionals," but it seems to me that the questions of religious pluralism will be posed in a new way in the coming decade, both in Europe's cities and in the relation between Christianity and world religions as religious-cultural systems. I hear the present message addressed to Christians and churches to be more like "we are not a part of a common project" than "let us go ahead." Such a message has long been heard, loudly and clearly, from Muslim countries with a total osmosis between political and religious powers.

Things do not get less complicated when we realize that the entire population of the globe *does* have a common project: the economic, social, and ecological crisis. Till not too long ago it was thought that ecology could be dealt with apart from the North-South economic crisis and the East-West political crisis. Now we know that there is only one, interlocking economic, sociopolitical, and ecological crisis, and that there is a common future (cf. the United Nations report "Our Common Future") or none at all.

There are no warrants for the belief that the new economic power that centers in Muslim states, in Japan, Singapore, and Seoul will act more prudently in terms of ecology and more justly toward the hungry and debt-ridden world than the United States and old Europe; the ecological clock ticks as the exploitation of the earth's resources goes on. Conflicts between world religions

---

A vague "spiritual humanism" is obviously not adequate to support a common global future.

---

won't help, and although Pope John Paul II has been ridiculed, by Catholics and Protestants alike, for his Assisi peace prayer with religious leaders, this event may signal what can be done in terms of interreligious dialogue for the foreseeable future. Such dialogue must concentrate on the penultimate and the search for some common ethical principles that will allow people of good will—within the religions and cultures and regardless of understanding of Ultimate Reality—to work for the survival of the planet.

A vague global-ideological "spiritual humanism" is obviously not adequate for the support of politics for a common future, and it may well be the task of interreligious dialogue to help clarify what the different religious traditions hold of elements that can make the faithful committed to invest in a future for grandchildren and for the endangered earth. For Christians it means putting the first article of the Apostles' Creed on the agenda.

Both in Europe and globally we need politics and societies (with all that is involved by way of lifestyles, educational patterns, government structures, and not least economics) concerned about peace *with* justice and conservation of the ecosystems. Nothing indicates, however, that the necessary shifts will come easily, and I do not think it is merely speculative to envisage a scenario where some Hindus, Buddhists, and Muslims will find themselves as much in opposition to predominant policies and politics of their respective religious-cultural societies as some Christians are in opposition to the rapacious economic systems of the West. A

common endeavor might be under way, but the reverse side of such bonding means added difficulties for struggling minority churches. Concepts cherished by dialogue theology, such as "inculturation" and "nation building" will have to receive renewed attention.

Evangelism and Proselytism

Whatever the outcome of shifts in the economic and political context for churches and mission, the foreseeable future means sharing the Christian faith in a torn and conflictual world, where most Christians do not have an option for the poor because they *are* poor. Most mission goes on in a context where basic needs are not met for most people; and most missionaries—the local congregations—have nothing to share but themselves and their faith; no material benefits. But it is equally true that resources in terms of funds and expatriate personnel still flow from first-world churches and mission groups, and that the structures for social outreach, justice education, church administration, and theological studies increasingly will need funding as the debt crisis increases the intolerable list of "most disadvantaged" countries in the southern hemisphere.

The ecumenical moratorium debate (the moratorium on expatriate personnel and funds from the North to third-world churches), died in the 1970s. As the economy of churches in Latin America, in black Africa, and in some Asian countries deteriorated in the 1980s along with the national economies, the ecumenical sharing of material resources from the North became more imperative.

The joys of common endeavors, and the miseries linked with struggles to overcome dependencies, I need not mention. The conflicts connected with having decision-making in poor churches and the funding in the first world will continue as long as the inequalities of the present economic system prevail. And these conflicts won't become easier to deal with as donor churches in the North learn that decision-makers with spiritual authority do not necessarily have a first-world, let alone a Vatican, address.

Demographic forces in conjunction with political and economic forces made the moratorium debate obsolete, even before it gained momentum. But another round of debate on a moratorium of a different sort is needed: a moratorium on proselytism. Nobody living in Central America or in Latin America's poverty-stricken countries is unaware of the rapid growth of all kinds of Protestant churches and parachurch groups. Most of that growth takes place not among those who have never heard the gospel, but among people who have been baptized into the Roman Catholic Church. I do not deny that evangelizing unchurched people may lead to their entry into a Christian community different from the one in which they first encountered the faith, but aggressive evangelization, aimed at reaching uprooted peasants and battered strugglers with crushed middle-class aspirations, will have to go by its proper name. It is proselytism, which is a corruption of authentic Christian witness.

The conflict, the pain, and the confusion is only augmented by the fact that many of the evangelization efforts are backed by ample economic resources making it possible to foster community and identity-building, personal and social development. Only the mindless can overlook the needs, and only the willingly deceived can pretend that the structures and economic resources of the Latin American majority churches will suffice to reach the population now being addressed by North Atlantic Protestant evangelization efforts. But is it really necessary to have women and men leave one church and join a different church or group as an integral element of sharing resources and helping the needy with food, education, sanitation, and jobs? The counterarguments are well known. They boil down to deeply felt convictions about the Bible, Christ, and salvation, and these convictions make it impossible to work ecumenically.

The problem of competitive efforts in evangelism will not easily be resolved. Conflicts about proselytism will grow in the United States as the Mainline churches intensify their outreach to Blacks and Spanish-speaking immigrants, especially to enable the implementation of quota systems in administrative procedures and structures. Many of these peoples have traditionally been members of Black Pentecostal and/or Roman Catholic communions. Proselytism among the unchurched and the steady stream of immigrants from Latin America—many of whom are already baptized—will be a continuing struggle and source of contestation.

There is little agreement among Christians on what precisely proselytism is, and hence little prospect of a constructive debate, let alone any solution to problems not even commonly acknowledged as problems. But even if Christians do not have a common language about the phenomenon, the reality articulated by the language still exists. I do not think that proselytism is a moot question; experience has convinced me that it is one of the rarely touched questions that influences—and will continue to influence—the ecumenical climate.

Ecumenism and Mission

It is at best hazardous to point to present trends that may have effect on the future. The risk of becoming a fool (and not merely feeling like a fool) lurks in every line of the writing. But having begun, let me add a few thoughts on possible historical shifts in Europe with consequences for global mission and ecumenism.

If perestroika continues in the Soviet Union, will European Anglicans, Catholics, Baptists, and Lutherans help the churches in the Soviet Union, first of all the Russian Orthodox Church, with *their* mission, in *their* way, to the peoples of the Soviet Union?

Will the churches of the Soviet Union be able to survive consumerism as well as they have survived persecution and martyrdom?

Will, for example, the Bibles in Russian language, so thoroughly needed, reflect the biblical canon as acknowledged by the Orthodox tradition, or will help come with conditions saying "accept *our* understanding of the canon and make do with the Old Testament and New Testament writings as we list them"? Will European Protestants be willing to let the churches in the Soviet Union go about evangelization and instruction of new members by way of worship and liturgies, liturgies and worship, and hours and hours in church? Or will all sorts of European Christians try to make the peoples of the Soviet Union part of their efficient mission project—with dire consequences for ecumenism?

If perestroika continues, will the churches of the Soviet Union be able to survive the onslaught of consumerism as well as they have survived the times of persecution and martyrdom? And what kind of help do consumer Christians in consumer countries really have to offer?

If perestroika continues and liberal freedoms (press, movement, freedom of religion) become more of a reality within the Soviet sphere of interest in Middle Europe, Mozambique, and Ethiopia—what will happen to the churches of these countries? Will everybody else try to smother them with unsolicited advice, or can one expect a restraint that will allow these churches to find their feet with regard to their own mission?

Conjectures, extrapolations from present facts, and mere guesses are just that, namely, conjectures, extrapolations, and guesses. Of one thing I am sure: nothing of what will be going on in the 1990s will be easy.

The Christian Message Versus "Modern" Culture

Lesslie Newbigin

Iam no prophet and no futurologist. I am impressed by the fallibility of all human attempts to peer into the future. As Christians our horizon of expectation is not any vision of what we might expect in the next decade or the next century. The horizon is firmly marked in our creed: "He shall come again in glory." That is sure; the rest is very fallible guess-work. For what it may be worth, let me try some guessing about the coming decade.

The Context

For 400 years the major thrust of Christian missions—Catholic and Protestant—has been bound up with the expanding economic and political power of Europe and North America. We are already witnessing a shift in the balance of power. The nations of the Pacific rim are now the expanding economic powers. They are investing on a massive scale in future growth. By contrast the affluent societies of Europe and North America are spending—probably beyond their real income—and investing little. As Jürgen Moltmann has said, they have hoisted a sign for all to see: "No future." And if one contemplates the life of these affluent societies, marked as it is by growing violence, drug addiction, and all the signs of the loss of meaning and hope, it is hard to see any future except collapse. Certainly anyone whose beliefs are shaped by the Bible can hardly fail to hear the word of God's dreadful judgment pronounced over that part of our world that calls itself "developed." Christians who come from the old "mission fields" to taste the life of the old "Christendom" are more and more deeply struck, and wounded, by the contrast between the

message they received from the early missionaries and the reality they now meet.

But the categorization of nations as first, second, or third world, popular since the 1950s, is no longer meaningful. More and more rapidly the whole world, and especially the expanding urban peoples of all the nations, are drawn into a single global network. The fantastic development of information technology in the past few years, development that continually accelerates, is locking more and more people into a single system—financial, economic, and ideological. The ideological battle between capitalist and Marxist systems becomes less and less significant. The power of Marxism seems to be waning, while capitalist societies show increasing signs of internal disintegration. Both are challenged by a resurgent Islam. Islam calls into radical question the assumptions that underlie both the capitalist and the Marxist ideologies.

The furor arising from the publication of Salman Rushdie's book *The Satanic Verses* has illustrated the internal weakness of the liberal democratic societies of the West. The question is posed whether or not the freedoms that these societies cherish as their most precious possession can be sustained in the absence of any ontological basis in the nature of God, and whether or not belief in God (or in any ultimate truth) can survive in a society that is incapable of understanding why blasphemy is a serious matter. My guess is that in the coming decade the prevailing relativism and subjectivism of our contemporary "Western" culture will be challenged more and more sharply by passionately held beliefs about fundamental realities, and that the sharpest of these challenges will come from Islam. That makes it imperative that we seek clarity about our message, about the content of the Christian mission.

The Content

It is instructive to look at recent history in this respect. The early missionary conferences (London 1888, New York 1900) did not think it necessary to discuss the message. Everybody knew what its content was; those taking part were agreed about a broadly evangelical Protestant faith. Edinburgh (1910) had no commission on the message as such, but devoted splendid scholarly resources to the question of the right Christian approach to each of the great religions. Jerusalem (1928) found it necessary to write a "Message," but that was so skillfully drafted by William Temple that it concealed profound disagreements, which surfaced during the succeeding years. The "Laymen's Report" (1932), J. H. Oldham's work on church, community and state (1934–37), and Hendrik Kraemer's "The Christian Message in a Non-Christian World" (1938) represented important and very diverse ways of spelling out the message. The debates at Tambaram failed to resolve the issues and for the next twenty years the questions raised by Kraemer about the relation of the gospel to the world religions dominated discussion. The questions posed at Jerusalem and by Oldham, questions about the relation of the gospel to secular society, were not generally perceived as central to the missionary message. Oldham was, in this respect, a lonely pioneer.

In a second phase the discussion of the message centered on the relation of gospel to culture. Perhaps it was at Bangkok (1973) that this issue was most prominent. Discussion of it was stimulated by the terms of the "second mandate" of the Theological Education Fund, with its emphasis on "contextualization." The weakness here was that the cultures discussed were almost

Lesslie Newbigin was for many years a missionary and bishop of the Church of South India in Madras. He is now retired in Birmingham, England, where he taught for several years on the faculty of Selly Oak Colleges.

always non-Western cultures. The question of the relation of the gospel to Western culture was seldom posed.

In a third phase (and of course these phases always overlap) the stress was upon the articulation of the message in relation to oppression and injustice. At the center of the missionary message was the "option for the poor." Perhaps the Melbourne Conference (1980) was the point at which the World Council of Churches' thinking on this was most prominent, but of course it was very widely present in many Protestant and Roman Catholic circles.

What is often not noticed about all these discussions is that they have been carried on in European languages and within the parameters of the worldview that has controlled these languages since the Enlightenment. To discuss "religions" as though they were a separable entity from the entire life of human communities is possible only in a society that has accepted the privatization of religion typical of modern Western culture. It is wholly inappropriate to the great world faiths. Equally, to discuss "culture" as a matter separable from human behavior as a whole presupposes that division of human life into the private and the public. There has not been a similar discussion of the question "The Gospel and Personal Behavior." And finally it must be said that

The prevailing relativism and subjectivism of... "Western" culture will be challenged more and more.

much of the discussion of the message in its relation to economic and social injustice has presupposed a Marxist analysis of the human situation rather than a biblical one. In the Marxist analysis human beings are divided into oppressors and oppressed. In the biblical understanding all human beings are both sinned against and sinners. That starting point leads to different conclusions.

What I think has been lacking, and what I hope the next decade will provide, is a serious and sustained effort to articulate the Christian message vis-à-vis this globally dominant Western culture, which has become the shared culture of at least the urbanized part of humankind. For this I think two things will be needed. One is the resolute effort to overcome the tragic split between "fundamentalists" and "liberals," so that there can be a coherent and credible appeal to biblical authority. Without this there is no *locus standi* from which the critical questions can be addressed to our culture. This split is itself a particular manifestation of the fundamental split in Western culture between a false objectivity and a false subjectivity, between a world of "facts" supposed to be available apart from the commitments of the knowing subject, and a world of "values" supposed to be purely a matter for the personal choice of the subject. When our minds are locked into this dichotomy, then we are compelled to choose between reading the Bible as a collection of "facts" and reading it as the record of subjective "religious experiences." In this situation, neither side can hear the other. We therefore need, second, the help of those whose minds have been shaped by non-Western cultures and who come to the Bible unencumbered by this dichotomy. At present this is difficult because the ablest theologians of the non-Western societies have been

trained in colleges and universities whose curricula were wholly in the Western model. I hope that the next decade may witness a fresh and resolute attempt to clarify the content of the Christian mission from a perspective that is not wholly controlled by the assumptions of Western thought.

And I hope that this re-thinking will lead to the correction of a defect that seems to me to be present in the whole debate about the missionary message during the past century. It has all been terribly Pelagian. Whether the emphasis was upon the saving of individual souls from perdition, or on the shaping of more truly humane cultures, or on the righting of social wrongs, the overwhelming emphasis has been upon missions as our program. From the New Testament I get a different impression. There, it seems to me, mission is an overflow of gratitude and joy. The center of the picture is not the human need of salvation (from sin, from oppression, from alienation) but God and God's immeasurable grace. So the central concern is not "How shall the world be saved?" but "How shall this glorious and gracious God be glorified?" The goal is the glory of God. The present decade has seen two world missionary conferences with the themes drawn from the Lord's Prayer: "Your Kingdom Come" (Melbourne 1980) and "Your Will Be Done" (San Antonio 1989). I would like to think that the next decade might see a world conference with the theme: "Your Name Be Hallowed."

The Community

Who will be the bearers of the mission in the 1990s? Who will be the missionaries? Modern missions began as the enterprise of groups of enthusiasts often with little backing from the churches. That has changed. The Tambaram meeting of 1938 posed the issue that could not be ignored. A church is no true church if it is not missionary, and missions are no true missions if they are not part of the life of the church. Faithfulness to that logic has led to measures—more or less effective—to integrate church and mission at national and international levels. What has not generally happened is integration at the level of the local congregation—and that is where it matters most. A congregation is not missionary just because it supports the work of a board or society; the question always is whether or not it is itself missionary, whether it exists as a witness to the people around it. I think that in the coming decade this question will be increasingly important. In the period when the major bearers of the Christian mission were churches in the rich and powerful nations, the main thrust was in the form of people and funds mobilized and sent by supra-congregational agencies. Yet even today the great numerical increases are taking place mainly through the quiet witness of members of congregations to their neighbors. I think this happens chiefly where church structures are flexible and the spontaneous generation of fresh centers of Christian congregational life is made easy. In this respect I think that we have still not properly learned the lessons of Roland Allen.

I am sure that international and intercultural missionary sending will continue and will be important, but I think that the main point of growth will be at the point where ordinary congregations are in contact with their neighbors. We are living in a time marked by skepticism about large organizations, even though (or perhaps because) the power of these organizations is increasing. Much of the liveliest Christian commitment is going into small groups, "base communities," "house-groups," and the like. This seems likely to continue into the coming decade.

To Make Strong Disciples

Join us as we learn to make strong disciples and foster Christian movements.

Discover the relevance and power of studies in mission and evangelism at Asbury's E. Stanley Jones School of World Mission and Evangelism.

The School offers a research tradition in discipling--the greatest single challenge for growing churches of the Third World and for churches in the secular West.

The School also features courses and research opportunities in theology and history of mission; church growth and mission strategy; mission, theology and indigenous Christianity; leadership and change agentry; communication and evangelism; urban mission and social reform; and Christian witness in the context of world religions.

- M.A. in World Mission and Evangelism
- Th.M. in World Mission and Evangelism
- Doctor of Ministry
- Doctor of Missiology
  Cooperative programs with The University of Kentucky:
- M.S.W. (U.K.) and M.Div. or M.A. (Asbury)
- Doctor of Philosophy (U.K.)

Faculty participating in Asbury's emerging research tradition in discipling include:

Ronald Crandall, P.Th.D., *Fuller*

Allan Coppedge, Ph.D., *Cambridge*

Steve Harper, Ph.D., *Duke*

Everett Hunt, Ph.D., *Chicago*

George Hunter, Ph.D., *Northwestern*

Reginald Johnson, Ph.D., *Edinburgh*

Donald Joy, Ph.D., *Indiana*

John Kilner, Ph.D., *Harvard*

Steve O'Malley, Ph.D., *Drew*

Darrell Whiteman, Ph.D., *Southern Illinois*

Mathias Zahniser, Ph.D., *Johns Hopkins*

THEOLOGICAL SEMINARY
WILMORE, KY   40390-1199

Contact Admissions for complete information: In continental U.S., call TOLL FREE 1-800-2-ASBURY. In KY (606) 858-3581, Eastern time Zone

And the strongest growing points are in the cultures that have not been shaped by "modern" Western culture. My guess, for what it is worth, is that it will be in the unspectacular and unheralded growth of small congregations, especially in the non-Western world, that the gospel will be communicated in the coming decade. But, at the same time, "modern" Western culture will continue to strengthen its grip on the life of human com-

> The central concern is not "How shall the world be saved?" but "How shall this glorious and gracious God be glorified?"

munities everywhere and—therefore—Christian churches that have so long accepted a syncretistic co-existence with the "modern" worldview will continue to bear the prime responsibility for articulating a Christian message for this particular culture. That remains a task which calls for the best intellectual and spiritual energies that we can bring to it.

Mission in Service of God's Reign

Barbara Hendricks, M.M.

Recently, I spent an afternoon of shared reflection with the first-year candidates of my community, the Maryknoll Sisters Congregation. We are a missionary institute of women religious who express our Christian commitment to world mission through formal profession of the vows of poverty, celibacy, and obedience. Our first year of formation has the goal of introducing the young woman to the key elements of our vocation: an apostolic, evangelical life of women religious lived out in the context of community with a simple lifestyle of insertion among the peoples of Africa, Asia, the Central Pacific, Latin America, and the United States. Within this context, the young woman experiences a shared life of interdependence and begins to explore and, it is hoped, to appropriate the call to transcultural mission with a specific option for the poor and marginated peoples in our contemporary world.

The friendly, relaxed atmosphere of the second-story living room of the formation house contrasted radically with the scene from the window overlooking a drug-traffic corner in a poor rundown neighborhood of Newburgh, New York. The house stands in a row of ancient, decrepit frame structures, typical of the inner-city sectors of the United States, and the street scenario it faces daily reflects one of the nation's biggest problems. But inside this particular house, new seeds for world mission are being planted and nourished.

Obedience to Mission

Our theme for the afternoon's study was the vow of obedience. We would be looking at "obedience" from the viewpoint of

Sister Barbara Hendricks served in Peru and Bolivia during the decades of the 1950s, 1960s, and the 1980s. In 1970 she was elected to serve as President of the Maryknoll Sisters Congregation, a position she held from 1970 through 1978. She now serves as co-director of the Maryknoll Mission Institute.

our call to mission, and each one of us came with a copy of our constitutions which govern our lives and our participation in mission. Our session began, however, not with the written word, but with the silent, as yet unspoken Word of God in each one's heart. After some minutes of silence each of us wrote a few words on a card, which expressed "obedience" for us at this point in our lives. Soon we were telling each other what obedience meant to us as Maryknoll Sisters or as candidates—seven women in the formation community and two of us who had come from our center at Maryknoll to facilitate the discussion. As each one shared her reflections, I noted the marked attentiveness that pervaded the group. Words and phrases began to flow around the room, giving me the impression that we were weaving a tapestry or composing a concerto. Obedience to Jesus and his mission was becoming a many faceted experience of brilliant colors and vibrant harmony with subtle nuances. Sometimes we had to grope for words in a "first language" and then search further to express the thought in our only common language, which was English. The phrases and words glided around us and settled deep inside us . . .

"discernment in community of God's plan for the world"
"faithfulness in listening to God"
"self-gift to follow Jesus in his mission"
"accompaniment of the poor in their journey"
"to be conquered and to follow"
"surrendering to love"
"to listen, to do, to answer—availability"
"openness, dialogue, discernment"
"fidelity to and within the struggle for transformation of the world"
"cooperation, openness, freedom in responding to the will of God even in suffering"

Each of us was being stretched beyond our narrow personal and cultural understanding and experience of Christian response. I glanced around me at each face and suddenly realized that this was potentially a missionary community for the twenty-first century.

In this warm, welcoming, family-style house in a drab, drug-infected neighborhood, we had an experience of "Mission in the 1990s" and beyond, into the third millennium of Christian mission. Women from six different parts of the world—Hong Kong, Japan, Korea, Peru, Tanzania, the United States—were breaking through barriers of culture, language, custom, tradition, and spirituality, dispelling age-old isolation, separation, and incomprehension in a simple sharing of God's Word alive in human hearts. We were helping each other to grow in faith, hope, and love, in and for a planetary community according to God's plan where all peoples are loved, and love, as sisters and brothers.

The Reign of God on the Earth

Being a missionary institute within the Roman Catholic tradition, the Maryknoll Sisters have been strongly impacted by Vatican Council II, and also influenced by the theological reflections of the Third General Assembly of the World Council of Churches at New Delhi in 1961. In the decade of the 1960s, many missionaries of all Christian traditions—Protestant, Anglican, Orthodox, and Roman Catholic—were already alert to the new winds of the Spirit moving in and through the pain and struggle of third-world peoples when the centers of North Atlantic Christianity began to articulate the challenges for renewal. We missionaries in Asia,

Africa, the Central Pacific, and Latin America responded to the new insights concerning the nature of the church and its mission in the second half of the twentieth century. We have read and studied many of the church documents published since the 1960s and realize that our "sending" churches are becoming increasingly aware of the church as *mission*.

For Catholic missionaries in Latin America during the 1960s it was a time of experiencing the emergence of a new kind of church and we with it. We studied the documents of Vatican II, especially "The Church" (*Lumen Gentium*), "The Church in the Modern World" (*Gaudium et Spes*), and "The Church's Missionary Activity" (*Ad Gentes*), and were filled with new theological and missiological insights. Paragraph 1 of "The Church" became an often-quoted and dearly loved refrain for us: "By her relationships with Christ, the Church is a kind of sacrament or sign of intimate union with God, and of the unity of all humankind. She is also an instrument for the achievement of such union and unity." This same document stated clearly that Christ, in order to carry out the will of the Father, "inaugurated the Kingdom of heaven on earth and revealed to us the mystery of the Father." This latter statement seemed especially significant

---

In a continent groaning in poverty, God's reign became the criteria for judging the effectiveness of mission.

---

to me, since it signaled a new and radical commitment to collaborate with human societies in addressing the critical problems of our times. In the reality of a continent groaning in poverty and longing for transformation, the understanding of "God's reign on the earth" would become the criteria for judging the effectiveness of mission presence and activity.

Perhaps the Vatican II document that affected us most was "The Church in the Modern World" because it challenged the church, as the people of God, to address critical global problems and to cooperate with others of goodwill in finding solutions to the growing situations of conflict and need. It ended its reflection with a call for the church to proclaim the gospel message of the kingdom and to unify under one Spirit all people of whatever nation, race, or culture by witnessing to the kingdom values and promoting honest dialogue, especially on the international level. There must be an effective presence of the church on the international scene because only in the context of a truly international community can the interdependence of all people and societies be accomplished by building a truly just and peaceful world.

What might otherwise have sounded like a restated triumphalism was reinterpreted and given another, deeper meaning by presenting a new, more humble image of the old church. The church is to be a servant to all peoples. As a servant church, while seeking the heavenly city, it must shoulder the responsibility of helping to reshape the earthly society where all nations will form a world community.

Vatican II helped us locate the missionary activity of the church within the center of the church's life instead of in its periphery for the "pilgrim church is missionary by her very nature." ("The Church's Missionary Activity," para. 2) When we look back on the development of mission theology over the postconciliar period we perceive a strong, steady movement from a church-centered concept of mission to a world-centered one. The symbol of the "kingdom" emerges as the determining element for our mission presence and activity. But the "kingdom" now discloses new meanings for us. It is not only the heavenly kingdom of eschatology but the beginning realization of God's reign on the earth, a reign of justice, peace, and love among all peoples. This is a rediscovery of the early church's expectations of the transforming power of God's Word as it is lived and proclaimed by the community of the disciples empowered by the Spirit.

The Consequences for Contemporary Mission

There are many consequences for contemporary mission in the light of a theology of mission centered on the symbol of God's reign on the earth. We are impelled to go directly to the full embodiment of the kingdom, Jesus himself and his teachings, for the criteria with which to develop our mission goals. In the light of the signs of our times, the pain and struggle in our world, to what kind of earthly reality does the kingdom point today?

Within the human situation, in the context of mission today, what is the basis for motivation, discernment, mutual support in our ministries, joy in our achievement, consolation in our failure, healing in our pain, and spiritual energy for continuing the mission of Jesus in its transforming task in our world today? Is not the overarching reality of the "communion of disciples" the only possible answer to these questions? From my own experience of mission in Peru in the decades of the 1950s and 1960s, and in Bolivia during the 1980s, I would say that the true communion of disciples is what consolidates the community sent in mission and energizes it for witness and service. Promotion of the kingdom and its values requires a reordered set of goals for mission institutes and agencies. Along with goals for ministries of service and the preaching of the Word, we had best list some goals for the achievement of an authentic quality of community life among missionaries themselves and in the communities that they form.

The quality of life of the missionary community, the way it embodies the message of Jesus as a "kind of sacrament or sign of intimate union with God, and of the unity of all humankind" is the indispensable requisite for mission, and it has been so from the beginning of Christianity. The quality of life in the community is of primary importance because anything contrary to this raises questions about the authenticity of the message, and the lack of community renders the message ineffective. It would appear that the heart of Christian mission is the community of the disciples gathered in the name of Jesus precisely for the purpose of gathering others to proclaim and make actual God's reign upon the earth. This quality of "see how they love one another" is what attracted new disciples, according to the Acts of the Apostles.

The Witness of the Missionary Community

The fidelity of the church, those called by Jesus as disciples, rests not on the numbers of people we baptize and incorporate into active membership but, rather, on the authentic following of Jesus Christ embodied in a local ecclesial community. The missionary presence and activity of a local Christian community will be judged by the quality of the life out of which it emanates and the salvific witness of loving relationships out of which it is energized for the preaching of the gospel. Perhaps the most impacting characteristic of the community's witness in the world today is servanthood. Authentic servanthood, lived out in humility and in a search for holiness, will dispose the missionary community for respectful dialogue, both ecumenical and interfaith, and for a service of liberation in a world steeped in materialism, consumerism, and secularism, and caught in the inhuman structures that reinforce the poverty of the vast majority of our brothers and sisters.

In the midst of all the anti-signs of our times, there are signs of hope. Among these we can name the growing awareness of the dignity, value, and self-direction of the human person and the relentless historical process that is reshaping the whole range of human relationships at every level of society; dominance/oppression, status/nonstatus, rich/poor, East/West, North/South, man/woman, and so forth. Faith is a gift and it is God the Giver who provides growth. The community in mission is called together to embody a sign that this historical process is directly related to God's plan. It does this by living the reign of God within itself and within its mission as a clarifying signal of prophetic announcement of what God is doing in our world and denouncement of the obstacles to its realization.

We know that the church is becoming a world church, although this is taking place in an awkward movement of steps forward and sliding backward. No one of us can see clearly the new shape of the church of the future, at either the universal level or the local expression. We cannot describe exactly what the role of missionaries from one local church will be in service to other churches. Yet theologians, mission administrators, and even we missionaries have taken to listing and describing such things as "Trends in Mission," "Mission in the Third Millennium," "Key Dimensions of Mission Today," "Mission in the 1990s," and so on. The majority of these reflections include the following elements in some form: Option for the Poor; Ecumenical and Interfaith Dialogue; Evangelization of the Human Person in Society; Evangelization of Cultures; Liberation of Peoples from Structures of Injustice, Poverty, Oppression, and Attitudes that Reinforce These Evils; and Accompanying and Empowering Local Christian Churches in Their Missionary Development.

There is also another major dimension of the future missionary outreach that is often named, sometimes implied, but generally not explicated as the basis for all the other major dimensions and the very core of all missionary activity since the early church—the witness of the life of the missionary community, that is, the quality of community life as witness of Jesus Christ and of the kingdom Jesus preached and inaugurated on the earth. Religious meaning is mediated most fully through persons who embody the message they preach. My belief is that the community in mission is the very heart of all the other challenges to mission in the 1990s. The sacramental quality of our witness as the community of those who believe in Jesus Christ, crucified and risen, as the definitive promise of the kingdom of justice, peace, and love has to be seen and touched by others so that it is an effective, visible, and living statement of our faith, hope, and love.

I belong to a missionary institute of women which was founded in the United States in 1912. In the past we have considered ourselves an American missionary movement. At present we see the growing internationality of our membership, which over the years has grown slowly to a ratio of 89 percent U.S. membership to 11 percent from other nations. We have experi-

INTERRELIGIOUS DIALOGUE
JUSTICE & PEACE
LIBERATION
INCULTURATION
INTERRELIGIOUS DIALOGUE

"Go out to the whole world;
proclaim the Good News to all creation."
MARK 16:16

Washington Theological Union Program in Mission and Cross-Cultural Studies

A concentration in mission and cross-cultural studies can be integrated into each of the following programs:

Graduate Degrees and Opportunities for Continuing Education

- Master of Divinity
- Master of Arts in Theology
- Master of Theological Studies
- Continuing Education Program

"To say Church is to say Mission . . .
Mission always expresses a concern
for the life of others."
—US Catholic Bishops, 1987

Mission Courses

A Christian Theology of World Religions
Approaches to Cross-Cultural Understanding
Catholic Evangelization in the United States
Global Spirituality: Individualism and Commitment
History of Mission
Liberation Theology: Interdisciplinary Perspectives
Missiology: Contemporary Perspectives
Native American Spirituality
Social Analysis and Recent Mission History
Soteriology: Is Jesus the only Savior?
The Relevance of African Christianity
The Church and the Hispanic Community

WASHINGTON THEOLOGICAL UNION

A Roman Catholic School for Ministry

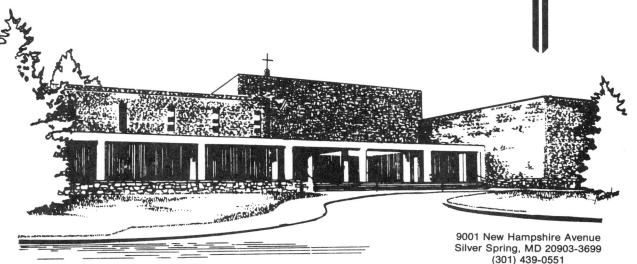

9001 New Hampshire Avenue
Silver Spring, MD 20903-3699
(301) 439-0551

enced lately the need to welcome consciously this trend among us as a sign of God's reign beckoning to the North Atlantic churches to open up to the cultural and spiritual riches of the rest of the peoples of the world at a time when those of us of Western Christianity need to be evangelized by the Christians of the South and of the East. We believe that this is a sign of the future of mission—a multicultural missionary community, where all nationalities, races, languages, spiritualities, and cultural traditions are valued, esteemed, and enriched by each other. This is no small challenge to both those of us from one of the most powerful nations in the world and those of us from Asia, Africa, Latin America, and the Central Pacific. It is, in fact, a challenge facing the whole church of the future.

The reorganization of missionary goals for the 1990s and beyond will, we hope, articulate the building of authentic global Christian communities as a priority for members of missionary institutes and agencies. This will be a call for conversion and liberation from all the destructive isolation and individualism that plague humankind in a time of chaotic transition toward a new era in history.

Toward the Globalization and Integrity of Mission

C. René Padilla

I can hardly think of the Christian mission in the 1990s without thinking of one of the most amazing changes that has been taking place since the beginning of this century, namely, the shift of the center of gravity of Christianity from the West to the two-thirds world. At least in part as a result of the modern missionary movement, millions and millions of people from the new nations, most of them poor, have made their debut on the stage of world Christianity. Of all the factors that will shape the life and mission of the church during the last decade of the twentieth century, this will undoubtedly be the predominant one. As Walbert Bühlmann has put it:

> The Third Church has arrived. This is *the* major event of Church history in the near future. To sum up in a few words: the first millennium of Christianity was the age of the First Church, the Church of the east; in the second millennium the stage was held by the Second Church, the Church of the west; the forms Christianity takes in the coming third millennium will in the main be determined by the Third Church, the Church of the southern hemisphere—Latin America, Africa, Asia." [1978:75–76].

The importance of this event should be taken to heart in relation to the following points of the missionary agenda.

Evangelization of the West

In this next decade much more will have to be done to find ways to communicate the gospel of Jesus Christ in the West. Not only in Europe but also in the United States many churches are "going out of business." By contrast, old religions like Hinduism, Buddhism, and Islam, and new religions and sects are

C. René Padilla lives in Buenos Aires, Argentina. He is General Secretary of the Latin American Theological Fraternity and editor of Misión, *a missiological magazine in Spanish.*

making their presence felt, sometimes with amazing force, in the religious scenario. In the United States, for instance, the New Age movement has a very impressive network for the dissemination of its ideas, values, and attitudes. According to a recent report, millions of copies of Shirley Maclaine's three autobiographies have been sold, 23 percent of the population believe in reincarnation, and 25 percent believe in a nonpersonal energy or life energy but not in a personal God. This phenomenon goes a long way to show that even in a secularized society people long for transcendence.

Are Christians equipped to respond to this situation? My impression is that most churches in Europe and the United States have no, or very little, evangelistic outreach. They are mostly catering to their own internal needs. Every time I visit the United States, for instance, I find all kinds of churches engaged in big building projects that absorb a very high percentage of their budgets. Moreover, not many churches seem to be concerned about, let alone prepared to face, the kind of issues that Lesslie Newbigin has insistently raised in his most recent writings, such as *Foolishness to the Greeks* (1986). One does not have to agree with every detail of his diagnosis of the spiritual problems of Western society to admit that the gospel has to be presented as public truth rather than as private religious opinion. Perhaps the greatest challenge that the church has to face in the West in this next decade is to witness to God's claim on the whole of life in the midst of a culture that has grown accustomed to the privatization of religion.

In his incisive sociological analysis of (North) American culture, Robert Bellah has pointed out that, in the United States, what he calls *ontological individualism*—"the idea that the individual is the only firm reality"—developed gradually as a part of the process of modernization beginning with the colonial period (1985:276). The net result of this idea is a culture of separation characterized by the fragmentation of life. The "social ecology," says Bellah, has been damaged, and unless it is repaired, "we will destroy ourselves long before natural ecological disaster has time to be realized" (1985:284). What has failed at every point, according to him, is integration; people have been too occupied with their own private interests—freedom, wealth, and power—but have neglected the common good. What is urgently needed is a social movement working for the transformation of the social world, the recovery of a social ecology in which individual interests will be linked to the common good, including the good of the poorest nations. "We have attempted to deny the human condition in our quest for power after power," concludes Bellah. "It would be well for us to rejoin the human race, to accept our essential poverty as a gift, and to share our material wealth with those in need" (1985:296).

From what Bellah says, two conclusions may be drawn. In the first place, it is quite clear that the restoration of the social ecology is one of the priorities of mission in the West. In the midst of a culture of separation, Christians are called to embody the love of God. Because of Jesus Christ's work of reconciliation through his death, no social movement is better qualified than the church to break down the barriers that separate people from one another. In the second place, there is a close connection between this restoration of the social ecology in the affluent countries and obedience to God's demand for justice to the poor. When Jesus told the rich young man to sell everything and give to the poor, he was thinking more about the spiritual need of the young man than about the material need of the poor. It is high time for Christians in the affluent countries to recognize their own poverty,

to be less introvertedly concerned about the maintenance of their church institutions, and to become far more involved in the struggle for the kingdom of God and God's justice. In the final analysis, the need of the hour is for a radical change from a privatized religion that reinforces the values and attitudes prevalent in society to a radical Christian commitment in response to Jesus' call to discipleship: "If anyone would come after me, he must deny himself and take up his cross and follow me" (Matt. 16:24).

No one would claim that privatized religion is unknown outside the West. All too often, privatized religion is one way in which the churches of the two-thirds world betray their missionary origin. Despite the persistent colonialist patterns of missionary work, however, much of the spiritual vitality that characterizes the churches in Asia, Africa, and Latin America is derived from the fact that they experience faith as inseparable from social life. Moreover, in the midst of poverty and oppression, they have intuitively perceived the relevance of the gospel to questions of justice and peace. That is why their nascent theologies generally maintain a very close link with socioeconomic and political reality. If in this next decade the Western churches, deeply affected by moral and spiritual decline, are to fulfill their missionary vocation, they will have to listen to the challenge posed by those theologies;

It is high time for Christians in the affluent countries to recognize their own poverty.

they will have to be willing to go beyond evangelism and become involved in the struggle for justice and peace in their own context and around the world. The evangelization of the West is inseparable from the rediscovery of the gospel as "good news to the poor."

Globalization of Mission

Most missionary-minded Christians today would agree that the gospel must be proclaimed in, from, and to all six continents. At least I would like to think that not many continue to view mission as moving from the "sending countries" in "the Christian West" to the "receiving countries" in the rest of the world. The trouble is that despite the wide recognition, *in theory*, of the need for a global outlook on mission, many Western missionary societies, *in practice*, continue to operate as if they were living in the nineteenth century. All the major policies are formulated and the most important decisions are made "at home," with little or no input from "the mission field." No measures are taken to have a wide cross-cultural representation on the board of the missionary society, nor to secure the participation of "national" leaders in the decision-making processes related to planning, programming, and evaluating. Paternalism still reigns supreme.

Never has the world been so small, nor have the means of communication across national barriers been so efficient, as at present. The scene is set for partnership in mission on a global scale. The kind of global partnership that is needed, however, will be possible only on the basis of honest recognition of cultural differences and real willingness to learn from one another across cultural barriers. It requires the renunciation of "a cultural imperialism which both undermines the local culture unnecessarily and seeks to impose an alien culture instead" (*The Willowbank Report*, para. 5).

One main obstacle to a globalization of mission based on partnership is the economic imbalance between churches in the West and churches in the two-thirds world. Because of it, all too often two assumptions are made: (1) that the role of the economically rich churches is not only to provide funds but also to design the missionary strategy, programs, and methods for the rest of the world; (2) that the role of the economically poor churches is simply to receive that which is generously given to them, for which they have nothing to offer in return. The net result of these assumptions is the perpetuation of both missionary colonialism and dependency. If such anomalies are to be corrected before the third millennium, Christian leaders everywhere during the 1990s will have to learn the meaning of interdependence within the body of Christ. They will also have to learn that, from the perspective of the kingdom, financial resources are never the most important thing that people in general, and the people of God in particular, can share among themselves. As David Auletta has put it, "All churches are poor in one way or another. All of them are involved in mission and are responsible for mission. All of them should be concerned for one another, help each other, share with one another their resources. All the churches should give and receive" (1974:87).

Integrity in Mission

In agreement with Johannes Verkuyl, a growing number of Protestant Christians today would affirm that "every evangelical (in the New Testament sense of that word) should be an ecumenical, and every ecumenical (in the biblical sense and also in the sense in which it was used by the pioneers of the ecumenical

> **Integrity in mission is not optional. It has to do with faithfulness to Jesus Christ.**

movement) should be an evangelical" (1989:56). Sad to say, however, the polarization between "evangelicals" and "ecumenicals" is not decreasing but increasing. This is the case, for instance, in Latin America, where this last decade has seen the development of two Protestant movements, the Latin American Council of Churches (CLAI) and the Latin American Evangelical Fellowship (CONELA), both of which are supposedly seeking to foster church unity. Verkuyl points out that, at a time when the Vatican is moving more and more in the direction of a "counter-reformation," many ecumenical Protestant churches are more willing to cooperate with the Vatican than with Protestant evangelicals (1989:56–57). If this situation seems ironic in Europe, it is far more so in Latin America, where the Roman Catholic "counter-reformation" is the order of the day and where Protestant evangelicals are still oftentimes regarded as intruders and their evangelistic efforts are seen as nothing more than proselytism.

A difference between "evangelicals" and "ecumenicals" is clearly illustrated by two important missionary conferences held in 1989: the World Conference on Mission and Evangelism convened by the World Council of Churches Commission on World Mission and Evangelism (WCC/CWME), in San Antonio, Texas, May 22 to June 1, and Lausanne II, the International Congress on World Evangelization convened by the Lausanne Committee for World Evangelization (LCWE), in Manila, Philippines, July 11–20. As in 1980, two conferences were separately planned to deal with questions related to the one-world Christian mission. The WCC/CWME conference was based on a prayer: "Your Will Be Done: Mission in Christ's Way." The LCWE conference, on the other hand, summoned the church to engage in world evangelization: "Proclaim Christ until He Comes: A Call to the Whole Church to Take the Whole Gospel to the Whole World." Behind the two gatherings were two different approaches to mission, one stressing the social dimension of the gospel and the other the need for conversion to Jesus Christ. Would two conferences need to be held if the two emphases were fully recognized for what they are—complementary aspects of the Christian mission?

Some of us who witnessed the birth of the Lausanne movement in the early 1970s had hoped that the Lausanne Covenant would become a rallying point for Christians concerned for integrity in mission. Sad to say, this hope was dampened by later developments through which the movement, not in theory but in practice, got away from the concept of holistic mission outlined in the Covenant. An influential (predominantly North American) group within LCWE was able to co-opt the Lausanne movement back into a posture that, in the "marriage" between evangelism and social responsibility, left the latter as a very underprivileged partner. Will the Lausanne movement honor the wholeness of the vision that emerged at Lausanne I, or will it simply reassert the one-sided approach of the U.S. evangelical establishment?

With or without the Lausanne movement, Christians everywhere in this coming decade will need to find practical ways to bring together evangelism and social responsibility, the personal and the public, faith and life. Integrity in mission is not optional. It has to do with faithfulness to Jesus Christ, the Lord of the whole of life.

References

Auletta, David, et al. 1974. *Misión nueva en un mundo nuevo*. Buenos Aires: Editorial Guadalupe.

Bellah, Robert, et al. 1985. *Habits of the Heart: Individualism and Commitment in American Life*. Berkeley/Los Angeles: Univ. of California Press.

Bühlmann, Walbert. 1978. *Courage, Church*. Maryknoll, N.Y.: Orbis Books.

Lausanne Committee for World Evangelization (LCWE). 1978. *The Willowbank Report*, Wheaton, Ill.: LCWE.

Newbigin, Lesslie. 1986. *Foolishness to the Greeks*. Grand Rapids, Mich.: Wm. B. Eerdmans Publishing Co.

Verkuyl, Johannes. 1989. "Mission in the 1990s." *International Bulletin of Missionary Research* 13, no. 2, pp. 55–58.

The Role of the People of God in the Divine Enterprise

Desmond M. Tutu

Preamble

It has taken me a very long time to note something that must be obvious to many people. In Leviticus God commands Moses to tell the people of Israel, ". . . be holy because I your God am holy" (Lev. 19:2ff). I should have realized long ago that this meant at the very least that God's people were expected to reflect the character of the God they worshiped, the God who had so graciously chosen them and delivered them from bondage. This fact was meant to provide the motivation for much of what they were expected to do in the area of ethics. They had to act in a way that was an *imitatio Dei*—they had to be generous and compassionate to the widow, the orphan, and the alien (Deut. 10:18, 19). They had to side with the powerless, the marginalized, because this is how God behaved toward them. They had to reflect this aspect of the divine character, they had to have the same concerns as the God they worshiped (Deut. 15:12–15, Lev. 19:9f, 19:3f).

This principle could be extended backwards to the time of creation, so that human beings, who were made in the divine image (Gen. 1:26–28), were expected to reflect God's character, conducting themselves in a manner that was intended to mirror the divine conduct and concerns. For us, the new people of God, the new Israel (Gal. 6:16, 1 Pet. 2:9f), the agenda of our concerns is set by God, who cares about us and all that he has created. Our activities should not therefore be a matter of random choice, as if we had an option in the matter. We do not. God gives the command and ours is to be obedient to the divine imperatives.

Priorities for Mission

Mission is a divine enterprise. We have the great privilege of

Desmond M. Tutu, Anglican Archbishop of Cape Town, South Africa, received the Nobel Peace Prize in 1984.

being invited to be God's collaborators, God's fellow workers (1 Cor. 3:9, Matt. 28:18–20, Mark 16:16ff), to accomplish God's goal when the kingdoms of the world will become the Kingdom of our God and his Christ and he shall reign for ever and ever. Amen.

God's intention was for all creation to exist in harmony and peace, as primordially represented by the idyllic existence in the paradise of the Garden of Eden, where there was no bloodshed, not even for religious sacrifice, for all in the garden were vegetarian (Gen.2–3). When that primordial peace and harmony were shattered, God's efforts were directed at recovering that which was lost—disintegration, alienation, and disunity were to become unity, togetherness, and harmony. And so we have the nostalgic vision of Isaiah II making a Hermann Gunkel speak of "Endzeit ist Urzeit"—"endtime would be as the time of the beginning"— or the unity in Christ spoken of in Ephesians 1:9ff. Jesus who would be our peace, breaking down all kinds of walls of separation (Eph. 2:14ff), making all peoples one people, fulfills the vision in Rev. 7:9ff.

We are thus exhorted to work for a just order where all of God's children will live full lives characterized by *shalom*. Concern for justice, righteousness, and equity is not fundamentally a political concern. It is a deeply religious concern. Not to work for

> ## The agenda of our concerns is set by God who cares about us and all that He has created.

justice and peace and harmony against injustice, oppression, and exploitation is religious disobedience, even apostasy. Thus one major mission priority is to work for the extension of what Jesus Christ called the Kingdom of God on earth characterized by *shalom*. The followers of Jesus would want to see the will of his Father being acknowledged and done on earth through zeal for the observance of human rights, to ensure that God's children would live harmoniously, as God intended them.

Earth should be a place where each is recognized as a person of infinite worth with inalienable rights bestowed by God, their Creator—where race, culture, religion, sex, and nationality are not used as means for denying some access to the resources God has made available to all. Where none is given an unfair advantage over others on the basis of something as extraneous as race, color, culture, sex, and so forth.

In proclaiming the Kingdom of God, we should seek to work for a recognition of the truth that we are created for interdependence, for togetherness, for fellowship, for family. We are meant for a delicate network of cooperation and interdependence (Gen. 2:18ff). That is the fundamental law of our nature, and when that law is flouted, all kinds of things go desperately wrong.

It is a religious imperative to be concerned about the arms race, about the threat of nuclear holocaust when we spend obscene amounts on budgets of death and destruction. A fraction of those amounts would ensure that God's children everywhere had a decent family life, with adequate housing and a clean supply of water, enough food, satisfactory education and health services in a community that ensured that children would not die prematurely from easily preventable diseases such as kwashiorkor, pellagra, TB, diphtheria, measles, and so forth.

This would be a society where people mattered more than things and profits, where cooperation and working together were at a premium and harsh competitiveness and horrendous self-aggrandizement were frowned on. We would be working for communities where compassion, caring, sharing, and gentleness were again admired and not despised; where human beings were valued for who they are—those created in the image of God, redeemed by Jesus Christ, sanctified by the Holy Spirit, and indwelt by God the Holy Trinity. People would be valued not because they were achievers or consumers, those who had *to do* something in order to matter, but simply for who they are. They are to be reminded that they are of more value than the sparrows, not one of which falls to the ground without the Father noting it (Matt. 10:29–31). The hairs of their heads are numbered and their names are engraved on the palms of God's hands. They count, they are loved with a love that does not change, that loved them before they did anything to deserve it, and that chose them before the foundation of the world (Jer. 1:4ff, Eph. 1:3ff).

We have been made to have dominion over the rest of God's creation (Gen. 1:26ff). Many are agitated that the biblical injunction appears to have been used as an excuse to exploit creation and God's natural gifts to us irresponsibly and wantonly out of our human arrogance. We are meant to have dominion, but it must be dominion as God would exercise it—compassionately, caringly, responsibly. It is sacrilegious to be so wantonly wasteful of God's creation, using up irreplaceable fossil fuels as if the supply were endless. It is a religious task to be concerned about ecology, about the purity of the air and water, about damage to rain forests and the ozone layer, about the greenhouse effect, about threatened species (both fauna and flora). These concerns will be mission priorities as we seek to make the universe more humane and "user friendly" and not red in tooth and claw.

In the face of much tragedy and catastrophe, when many wonder whether life is just sound and fury signifying nothing, we must continually stress that there is meaning in it all, that it is a drama that has point. There is a denouement. It is the story of a God who has not remained aloof but is Emmanuel, God with us (Isa. 7:14), who has heard our cries, who knows our suffering, and who has come down to deliver (Exod. 3:7f). The story is of one who, though equal with God, did not reckon this something to be snatched at, but emptied himself, took on the form of a servant, and became obedient even unto death, yea, the death of the cross. One whom God has highly exalted, giving him a name above every name, that at the name of Jesus all knees should bow for the glory of God the Father (Phil. 2:5–11).

The story calls us to go forth into all the world to make disciples of all people, baptizing them in the name of the Father and the Son and the Holy Spirit (Matt. 28:19f). We are being taught how to live with a bewildering but glorious plurality of peoples, cultures, faiths, and ideologies in a world that is shrinking rapidly into a global village where we are all neighbors.

When will we learn to live as brothers and sisters? It is only then that we can survive; otherwise, as Martin Luther King, Jr., warned, we will perish as fools.

Recovering the Biblical Worldview for Effective Mission

Neuza Itioka

When Dr. Wilbur Pickering and his wife reached the upper Amazon in 1963 to begin their missionary career, they knew exactly what they would do. He would begin translating Scripture portions into the language of the Apurinã Indians. He knew these primitive people were animists. Demons were central to all their activities. Birth, death, marriage, child rearing, fishing and food gathering were all in some way related to their spirit world.

As Dr. Pickering related the task to his thorough training in theology, linguistics, and anthropology, he was confident he could do the job. What he did not realize was that his mission board, in a peculiar kind of naïveté, had sent him to his field unprepared to understand or deal with the dark spiritual realities of an animistic culture.

One day as Dr. Pickering was walking through the village, he suddenly fell to the ground with acute abdominal pain. The pain subsided and he got up, only to be thrown to the ground with the same pain. By now, Indian bystanders were laughing at him. Dr. Pickering got up and went on his way, completely baffled by his strange experience.

Later, to his astonishment and shame, Dr. Pickering realized he had been attacked by demons. The laughing Indians knew very well what was going on, even though he did not. Forced to rethink the reality of the spirit world, he opened his Bible and began a serious study of supernatural power. Later, he lamented that he had not been as effective in evangelizing the Apurinãs as he might have been, had he been trained to work with the spiritual

Born in Brazil of Japanese parents who went to Brazil as lay missionaries to the large Japanese population in Brazil, Neuza Itioka is on the training staff of AVANTE, a cross-cultural missionary sending agency in São Paulo. She is also a missionary of O.C. Ministries. She has a Doctor of Missiology degree from Fuller Theological Seminary and has published two books in Portuguese.

powers he encountered there.[1]

The problem Dr. Pickering confronted firsthand is not restricted to primitive, animistic cultures. It is also at work in the secularized, atheistic culture of a country like Uruguay. "Training in spiritual warfare is the most important preparation we can have for missionary work here," says Celso Thomanzini, a young missionary working there. "In evangelization and church planting we must understand how to deal with supernatural evil power."

Over the years the Uruguaian government has systematically abolished Catholicism as the official religion. Today Uruguaians boast that they are the first truly secular society in Latin America. They are proud of the "intellectual objectivity" that has made religion the least important area of their lives.

Looking beyond the official claims of secularization, however, the careful observer sees another reality: There is a presence of spiritual death, oppression, and indifference. Even though they have been taught that their beliefs and practices are shameful, spiritist "healers" recognize the hunger of a so-called secular people and carry on a clandestine ministry.

The Protestant and Evangelical churches in Uruguay are very small. But a small group of missionaries has begun to engage in spiritual warfare through fasting, prayer, and addressing the powers

---

There would be neither mission, nor church, nor salvation if the Son of God had not triumphed over the powers of evil on the cross.

---

of darkness. They do not face primitive animism, as did Dr. Pickering in the Upper Amazon, but they confront the same principalities and powers in an urban guise. In a very short time they have been able to establish a church in what was thought to be a very unresponsive area.

Spiritual Evil Power

Certainly one of the most important issues worldwide missions must face in the 1990s is how to confront the destructive supernatural evil forces that oppose the missionary enterprise. For too long the western church has tended toward an intellectual expression of its faith, failing to face realistically the supernatural manifestations it must confront.

A major failing of much of the church in the past and today is the loss of a biblical perspective of reality. What is our mission? Is it not to rescue people and nations and lands from the power of Satan, bringing them to acknowledge the true God in submission to his lordship? Because of this loss of perspective, many missionaries find their work does not bring about the results they had hoped for.

Nature of Christ's Work

If we consider the nature of the work of Christ and the call of his

church to give continuity to this work, we will agree that we must focus on what Jesus came to do—destroy the work of the devil (1 John 3:8). How did Jesus do this? The gospel tells us he listened to the Father and obeyed him. He spoke the words of the Father and ultimately destroyed the power of darkness on the cross. In fact, Jesus came to die on the cross so that he might put to shame the principalities and powers, to disarm them and make a public example of them, triumphing over them in him (Col. 2:14, 15).

There would be neither mission, nor church, nor salvation if the Son of God had not triumphed over the power of evil on the cross. By this act Christ overthrew the old world system under Satan and established a new spiritual system under his lordship.

The church of Jesus Christ is called to do the same: to participate in building this new spiritual order, to rescue humanity from the old system. This task involves the supernatural work of a triune God in the persons of the Father, the Son, and the Holy Spirit. It is only with their involvement that people will be rescued to become a new creation.

Western Worldview vs. Biblical Worldview

In a gradual and subtle way, the western church has identified itself with a rationalistic, scientific, materialistic worldview that leaves little room for the supernatural. Even when humanistic anthropologists and sociologists began to investigate supernatural manifestations[2], Christians failed to take note. How ironic it is that it is Christians who ignore or at best only pay lip service to supernatural reality in the world today.

Have we forgotten that Paul said our struggle is not against flesh and blood, but against principalities and powers? Do we believe he was speaking only of human political organizations and institutional power?

Our perception in this area is so dulled that only a few have pursued a careful study of the forces behind the scene controlling human, political, social, and economic institutions.[3] This power must be recognized as a spiritual evil power that controls the whole world (1 John 5:18).

Modern science is said to rest upon a faith that is the fruit of the long schooling of Europe in the worldview of the Bible.[4] But our western Christian worldview is incomplete. For our convenience, we have abolished the spirit world and mistakenly concluded that the biblical worldview deals only with the rational. In truth, the biblical worldview includes the supranatural, with God, angels, demons, and people moving in the same realm.

The result of this inadequate view of spiritual reality is that missionaries implant a secularized kind of Christianity.[5] We did away with what we called the superstitions of ignorant, uneducated people. As a result, many converts were forced back to their old ways of life because there was no place in their newly adopted Christian worldview for the supernatural power they saw at work on a daily basis. This is tragic because it is at this juncture that the Holy Spirit is supposed to be at work.

Unfortunately our western theology and missiology have not taken seriously the person of the Holy Spirit. Part of the problem began with the Reformation. In reaction to the mystical elements of Roman Catholicism, all mystical approaches to faith were discouraged. Supernatural manifestations of God and his power were no longer expected.

But our difficulty lies not only in the problem of an inadequate worldview. Perhaps a more crucial problem is one of discernment. Is it possible that we are so comfortable with conventional theological training that we have not taken seriously the spiritual realm that is so real to the people we wish to reach?

Discernment and the Holy Spirit

It is worth noting that Jesus as the Son of Man confronted Satan only after a personal infilling of the Holy Spirit at baptism. Only then did this same Spirit lead him to face the temptations recorded in Luke 4.

It becomes clear, then, that a correct perception of spiritual reality is inextricably linked to pneumatology. Most notably the Pentecostals, and more recently the Charismatics, have discovered this truth. But for most mainline denominations, the work of the Spirit is still restricted to salvation, sanctification, and token recognition in the singing of the Doxology.

To the extent that the church presented the Bible in a way that emphasized the letter and ignored the Spirit, a living Christ who intervenes today in human affairs was put aside. Fear of fanaticism became a constraining factor, as did distorted views of the person and work of the Spirit. As a result, it was easy to deny a contemporary manifestation of the Holy Spirit and to relegate his gifts and ministries to apostolic times.

But how can we speak of evil spiritual power without considering the power of the Holy Spirit? Demonology and pneumatology are inseparable if we are to rightly discern between spiritual and natural forces at work in the universe.

Third World Context

Today many Third World countries are experiencing acute social, economic, and religious problems. Poverty, corruption, violence, idolatry, and bargaining with the devil are one side of the coin. On the other side are materialism, consumerism, the exploitation of the poor, the weak, and the outcasts. Our temptation is to focus the gospel on this second set of problems to the exclusion of the first.

However, if the church of Jesus Christ could discern the true causes of these catastrophic woes, we would turn our efforts to a struggle against principalities and powers in heavenly places. It is here that we find the roots of these problems, in a humankind that offends God by not glorifying him, by not giving thanks to him. Nations have become futile in their thinking; their senseless minds have become darkened by every kind of idolatry and witchcraft (Rom. 1:21).

Brazil, with its openly practiced witchcraft and demonism, is a good example of the interplay between social, economic, and political upheavel. For millions of Brazilians, demons who represent spirits of the departed are gods to be worshiped and appeased. This practice contributes significantly to Brazil's inability to realize its real potential as a nation. While Brazil is the seventh world power in terms of economy and fourth in food production, poverty increases and the gap between the upper and lower classes widens. Our situation as a nation reflects the gods we have chosen to worship.

What is true of Brazil is also true of other Third World countries. In Uruguay, when the veneer of Christendom is stripped aside, one finds millions who have either a mystic or animistic worldview. Africa and Asia, too, are power oriented societies. The "spirits of the departed" are part of everyday life. Divination, healing, and witchcraft are commonplace as individuals and families experience spiritual oppression and affliction.

If Christian missionaries are to be effective in these cultures, their ministry must be contextualized. Conventional prayer will do little to conquer these peoples, tribes, and nations for Christ. Our preaching and teaching cannot include only the rational and intellectual. It must go beyond, to deal with spiritual powers. Oscar Culmann points out that in the New Testament the spirit world is a prominent factor. Wherever Jesus ministered, the presence of the supernatural was seen.[6]

This lack of perspective influences even our prayer life. Prayer is not just a way of asking God to meet our needs. It is also a way to call God to engage in battle with principalities and powers. Ephesians 6:18 takes on new meaning in this light. After Paul describes the Christian armor, he suggests that the Christian life is a continual struggle on a spiritual level, a struggle to work in partnership with God against spiritual powers. "God limits some of his activities in response to the prayers of His people. If they do not ask, he will not act. Heaven's desire awaits our stimulation and initiative in revealing to him our will and then to desire and pray that this will be brought to pass."[7]

We must also contextualize our preaching. Paul said his preaching was not with "wise and persuasive words, but with

> ## To reach people who coexist daily with the supernatural, we need the powerful presence of the risen Christ.

a demonstration of the Spirit's power . . . " (1 Cor. 2:4). If we only address the minds of people to change their way of thinking, replacing old doctrines with new doctrines, we miss the point. This is why the apostle Paul went to Corinth to demonstrate the power of the Spirit (1 Cor. 2:4).

The rational, intellectual approach we have used for so long brings only new information, a new way of thinking. What we need to reach people who coexist daily with the supernatural is the powerful presence of the risen Christ. He is the missionary and evangelist par excellence. Without his intimate involvement, we have no mission and there will not be transformation in the lives of people.

And how do we invoke the presence of the risen Christ? The one who glorifies Jesus as Christ is the Holy Spirit. He is the one who leads us into truth (John 16). He is the empowerment behind effective missionary activity.

Changing World

The power of evil has been with us since the Garden. But now we are seeing a rapid change in spiritual values on an international level. Britain and the United States, nations that have taken Christianity to the ends of the earth, are now countries where sophisticated forms of witchcraft and satanism are widely practiced. It is said that there are 10 million witches in the United States alone.[8]

We must take the European expansion of neopaganism very seriously, for it alters the view of history, man's wholeness, and his relationship to nature and life and death. More importantly, it is a manifestation of evil power that enslaves people who have

When Your Calling is Missions...

Call us!
1-800-888-0141

rejected Christianity. For example, some statistics show that in France the number of witches exceeds the Protestant population.[9]

What we are seeing is a reversal of worldviews. While the northern hemisphere is becoming more pagan, the southern hemisphere is being evangelized, won for Christ, and the church is growing. Does this mean that we are more biblical or that our theology is more correct? Clearly, if we can release the grip that western rationalism has on us and let the people in the southern hemisphere regain their worldview, they will be closer to biblical thought patterns than we might imagine.

The phenomenon we now observe is that the older sending countries are themselves becoming mission fields. The western church is not growing as fast as the Third World church. Rational Christianity is being challenged by power-oriented religions such as witchcraft and satanism.

What must happen if the church is to witness effectively for Christ in cultures built around the concept of spiritual power? We must acknowledge in a new way the realities of the spirit world presented in the Bible, and we must have the ability to discern this spiritual reality when it is present. Only then, as we employ spiritual weapons in the power of the Holy Spirit, will the church do the job it was called to do: deliver people from the power of darkness and transfer them to the kingdom of his beloved Son (Col. 1:13).

Notes

1. Gilberto Pickering, *Guerra Espiritual* (São Paulo; Casa Publicadora Assembléia de Deus, 1988).
2. See Roger Bastide, *The African Religions of Brazil* (Baltimore: Johns Hopkins University Press, 1987).
3. See Watchman Nee, *Não Ameis o Mundo*, 3d Brazilian, ed. (São José dos Campos: CLC Editora, 1986), p. 10.; René Padilla, "Evangelism and the World," *Mission Between the Times* (Grand Rapids, Mich.: William B. Eerdmans Publishing Co., 1985); Walter Wink, *Naming the Powers* (Philadelphia: Fortress Press, 1984) and *Unmasking the Powers* (Philadelphia: Fortress Press, 1986). In these two books, Wink has carefully studied the principalities and powers. He analyzes the biblical use of the language of powers and analyzes the powers behind human, social, political, and economic institutions.
4. Lesslie Newbigin, "Can the West be Converted?" *International Bulletin of Missionary Research* 11, no. 1 (1987): 2–7.
5. Lesslie Newbigin, cited in Paul Hiebert, "Flaw of the Excluded Middle," *Missiology: An International Review* 10, no. 1 (1982): 44.
6. Michael Green, *I Believe in Satan's Downfall* (London: Hodder and Stoughton, 1980), p. 81.
7. Arthur Mathews, *Nascidos para a Batalha* (São Paulo: Editora Vida, 1987), p. 16.
8. Overseas Crusades Research Department, Memo from Dr. Larry Keyes, President, to OC missionaries, dated April 15, 1988.
9. Ibid.

The Pillars of Mission in Asia

C. G. Arévalo, S.J.

Agenda for Mission

The last two decades have produced so many discussions on the theology of mission and of the church's missionary activity, so much soul-searching and debate on the role of missionaries and on the tasks of Christian mission as we move toward the third Christian millennium, that we can only repeat, or pick up and choose from, the positions already taken and the agenda already drawn up by countless conferences, seminars and individual theologians. The essays already published in the INTERNATIONAL BULLETIN OF MISSIONARY RESEARCH on "Mission in the 1990s" have done us the service of summing up much of the enormous contemporary literature on the subject of Christian mission and the questions it raises today.[1] This contribution thus cannot be expected to say anything new. It will try instead to present "Mission in the 1990s" from a rather specific Roman Catholic viewpoint and from a definite context: East and Southeast Asia.

For twenty years, Roman Catholic bishops and theologians have struggled with the subject of Christian mission—more precisely with the mission of the church—in what might be called the "FABC region" (Federation of Asian Bishops' Conferences), that part of Asia that Europeans call "the Far East." ("Far from whom?" the renowned Filipino historian, Horacia de la Costa, used to ask.) The years following the Vatican Council II saw in Latin America the remarkable emergence of CELAM (Consejo Episcopal Latinoamericano) and the significant movements in theology and ecclesial life and praxis that the names of Medellín and

C. G. Arévalo, a Filipino priest of the Society of Jesus, teaches ecclesiology and theology of mission at Loyola School of Theology, Ateneo de Manila University, Philippines. He served as a member of the Papal International Theological Commission (1974–1986) and has been a theological consultant of the Federation of Asian Bishops' Conferences since its foundation.

Puebla evoke. In a lower-profile way the FABC assemblies and workshops represent in East and Southeast Asia what CELAM II and CELAM III have meant for the churches in Latin America. It is appropriate, therefore, to give readers a summary of FABC thought and directions on the theme of Christian mission.[2] It is my conviction that mission in Asia, as far as the Catholic Church is concerned, will be in continuity with these directions, that the 1990s will spell out these orientations in more concrete ways and deepen the theological understanding of these areas of ecclesial thought and practice.[3]

1. Always the point of departure in the thought and texts of the FABC conferences has been the vision of a "new world being born" in Asia since the end of the colonial period in our part of the earth. In "this vast and varied, restless and swiftly-changing world" of nearly three billion people (almost two-thirds of humanity), we see an ever-widening, ever-increasing search, "new today in its breadth, restlessness and urgency," for the reshaping of national societies and human communities "in the midst of so much social change, conflict and struggle, suffering and oppression, inhumanity and death." This search "defines the turbulent history of our time." FABC documents clearly and explicitly affirm that the church's missionary proclamation and activity must be in close dialogue with the realities of this context and must seek to respond to the "signs of the times."[4]

This perspective, on the part of Roman Catholic Church leaders in Asia, is a relatively new one. Vatican II, especially its pastoral constitution *Gaudium et Spes*, provided the necessary intervening moment toward the acceptance of this perspective. If we may draw wisdom from a perceptive remark of Cardinal Newman, however, it will take another generation before this point of view becomes universally accepted by church leadership. But the establishment of this new perspective is henceforth irreversible and decisive.

2. From 1971 onward it has been affirmed—most clearly by the FABC General Assembly of 1974 at Taipei—that the "basic mode of mission in Asia" must be dialogue. *Missionary* dialogue, of course. We must explore the interface of the Gospel's meanings and values with the realities of Asia and its many peoples—its histories and cultures, religions and religious traditions, and especially its "poor masses" in every country. These realities—cultures, religions, life-situations of poverty—make up the ambience and context wherein the Gospel is to be proclaimed; these realities define the "place" for the localization of the church and the inchoate "*real*-ization" of God's kingdom.

This overarching program of dialogue with the cultures (i.e., inculturation), with the religions and religious traditions (i.e., interreligious dialogue), and with "our peoples, especially the poor multitudes in Asia" (i.e., development/liberation), has been the thematic background of both the pastoral and missionary activity of the local churches of Asia in the past twenty years. In the 1979 International Mission Congress (Manila) it was used as the overall framework for reflection on mission and the tasks of mission in the 1980s. For the 1990s these dialogues remain the headings under which the concerns and activities of Christian mission are collocated. It is in the endeavor to bring these dialogues into life and practice, and in the ongoing reflection on the processes they have initiated, that the way of theologizing on mission must surely be constructed in the decade to come.

3. The "acting subject" of this missionary work and dialogue must be, concretely and in the first instance, the "local church."[5] The local churches and Christian communities constitute the responsible historical subject of mission today in Asia (again, in the first instance). It is they who can discern and work out the way the Gospel is best proclaimed, the church set up, the values of God's kingdom realized in their own place and time. The local Christian community "becomes church" largely through interrelationship with the milieu that is its place and context of mission.

4. The local church means the entire Christian community, the "entire people of God" in this given time and place. Here the participation in the church's missionary activity of laypeople is especially to be stressed. This total ecclesial community is, in the first instance, "the self-acting and self-realizing subject of the church's mission"; the proclamation of the Gospel by word, witness, and work, within the concrete realities of a people's life, is a common task shared by all Christians and involving the entire community of faith.

Once again, if the language is not new, the living out in practice of these principles *is* new and has hardly begun to get off the ground. Here is where one of the most important realities, perhaps the most important reality that has emerged in Christian churches in Asia in the past twenty years, must be named: the grassroots ecclesial communities, or Base Ecclesial Communities (BEC), involving Christians "where they are and where they are at." We may note that although the BEC notion has gained very wide attention and encouragement in official texts and documents, the concrete emergence of BEC in Asia is only at the beginnings, except perhaps in a few areas (e.g., on Mindanao island in the Philippines). Similarly, the wider, fuller participation of laypeople in ministries, called for repeatedly in the past twenty years, is only in its early stages, even if these beginnings are significant enough to invite widespread attention and advocacy.[6]

5. "[In] practice . . . mission is no longer, and can no longer be, a one-way movement from the 'older churches' to 'the younger churches.' . . . Every local church is and cannot be but missionary. Every local church is sent by Christ and the Father to bring the Gospel to its surrounding milieu and to bear it also to all the world. For every local church this is a primary task. . . . [Every] local church must be a sending church, and every local **church (because it is not on earth ever a total realization of the church) must also be a receiving church. Every local church is** responsible for its mission, and co-responsible for the mission of its sister-churches. Every local church, according to its possibilities, must share whatever its gifts are, for the needs of other churches, for mission throughout mankind, for the life of the world."[7]

These words, written in 1979, have already been remarkably verified. Exact figures still have to be gathered, but from general information we know that already "missionaries from the two-thirds world" have taken up the tasks of mission in all continents, and "the internationalization of the missionary movement is the great new fact of our time."[8]

6. "The proclamation of Jesus Christ is the center and primary element of evangelization, without which all other elements will lose their cohesion and validity. In the same way, evangelization will lead to gathering together a believing community, the church."[9]

Bishops and pastoral leaders in the FABC region, and the theologians who work most closely with them, have never wavered in the primary role they give to the proclamation of the Gospel and of Christ. It is no secret that much theological writing in our area in the past few years has raised radical questions about the uniqueness of Christ in the history of salvation. A good deal of current thought on this matter focuses on "the myth of Christian uniqueness" thesis. If it is true that a few Asian theologians (in agreement with some of their Western counterparts) propose a full-blown pluralistic theology of religions whose bottom-line is finally a parity of religions, still the Asian Roman Catholic bishops in their statements on mission and interreligious dialogue have been consistent in holding on to the "traditional" view on the uniqueness of Jesus Christ as the one mediator of God's salvation in history.

The agenda outlined above received remarkable confirmation in the SEDOS Seminar on the Future of Mission (Rome, March 8–19, 1981), which identified the directions foreseen for the coming decades as proclamation, dialogue, inculturation, and liberation of the poor. The final conclusions insisted on "the central place of the Local Church." Whether or not the FABC texts had a strong influence on the SEDOS Seminar is not really important; what is significant is the near-total agreement regarding the directions for the future of mission.[10]

The Doing Remains

In the theology of mission, then, it is clearly on this same FABC itinerary that the interaction of praxis-reflection-policy-action must move. And "all the doing remains."[11]

Inculturation has been very much present in theological discussion since the 1960s, but its implementation has not really

---

> ## Mission today must be about the creation of Christian community.

---

moved forward in a genuinely significant or decisive way. The *liberation theology* breakthrough and subsequent vigorous debate on it now have been in the forefront of attention for more than fifteen years. This movement without doubt has been a major dimension of the ecclesial/missionary life of our time; the contribution of the Latin American churches has been invaluable for a rethinking of mission. Liberation theology's energies are not spent, and for the decade to come we await continuing development and greater participation by other sectors (Asia, Africa, etc.).

Interreligious dialogue has gradually but steadily been moving toward front-and-center in the past few years. It will surely assume larger proportions in the coming decade. The debate on "the myth of Christian uniqueness" is already productive—not only of unsettling questions—but of a deepening reexamination of the person and the message of Jesus and of the salvation found in him. In this discussion of the very meaning of Christianity, the caution must be repeated that constant contact needs to be maintained with those *actually engaged* in missionary life and action and with "practicing believers" in other religious traditions. A mere exchange of ideas largely elaborated in academic circles begs to become a game of chess instead of a genuine service to mission in our time.

The Asian Theological Advisory Commission (TAC) of the Asian Bishops' Conferences, constituted in 1985 to advise the FABC, after informally sounding out the Asian episcopal conferences to find out what the pastoral leaders in the region believed

were the most crucial and most urgent theological concerns, placed two themes—the theology of interreligious dialogue, and the theology of the local church—as the top items on their agenda.

The concern for the local church is an attempt to understand the situation of church communities on various levels in the present period of the church's history in Asia. In many ways it is an effort at coming to grips with what the mission and task of each local Christian community must be, in the most concrete manner possible, as it tries to live the imperatives of the Gospel and insert the Gospel's meanings and values in the human milieu whose common history it shares. This will obviously mean a deepening understanding, not only of the milieu of proclamation, witness, and service, but of the concretion (or incarnation) of the Gospel's meanings and values in a given time, place, history, and culture. Hence the concern that inculturation and dialogue, as well as human and societal development and liberation, become concrete in "the living out of its own particular mission, by the local church." The fulfillment of Christian mission is the way to self-realization of the church as authentic bearer of the Gospel in its being and life, in its own place and time.

> Our planning for mission activity should start from below. What we should do in a particular situation cannot be determined *a priori* from above. It should be the fruit of an analysis of the situation, of the kind of people with whom we are working, of their real needs. It is by involving ourselves with them and experiencing life with them that we shall be able to discern the will of God in that situation. Mission is not bringing God to a place where he is not present, but helping people to discover and listen to God who is there, perhaps hidden or dimly perceived or seen differently, but who is calling them all the time towards a dialogue leading them to fuller life.
>
> Such a mission can be best accomplished only by a local church. . . . Each church is on mission and is co-responsible for mission all over the world. So instead of the more familiar concept of "foreign mission" we will have to be accustomed to the concept of collaboration in mission. . . . The vision of the Church universal as a communion of local churches will also be manifested as a communion in mission.[12]

Some Enduring "Musts" for Mission

At this point I would like to recall yet older, more traditional things. They center around the spirituality of mission.

1. The thrust of grassroots ecclesial communities is a return to the most fundamental of Christian basics: *koinonia*, the trinitarian life experienced and shared with the community of faith, hope, and love. Mission today must be about the creation of Christian community, about the building up of human solidarity, beginning on the grassroots level. Hence the continuing importance of "base communities" and what they concretely mean for communion and participation.[13]

The realization of community, sociologically speaking, will differ from place to place, from society to society, from culture to culture, from "level to level." Community is not a univocal term, and its realization will take on diverse concrete expressions. Perhaps the word *solidarity,* so frequently in the vocabulary of John Paul II, best translates what is meant here.[14]

2. In his mission letter issued in 1975, Pope Paul VI spoke of the need of radical Christian witness for our time: the witness of totally given, self-sacrificing love. In the surfeit of words in our age, he said, only those teachers who teach by deed will be

heard, or who join the witness of their lives to their words.[15] This will be more valid, if possible, in the 1990s than it was in the 1970s. The names of Archbishop Romero and Mother Teresa most readily come to mind. In the history of Christian mission, the witness of life has always been the most effective vehicle for the Gospel. If this sounds like a platitude, it is a platitude that bears repeating today, when the outreach and power of ministry in media would seem sometimes to be saying something to the contrary.

3. Lastly, and in the same vein, we must affirm what a work on the theology of mission published not too long ago calls "mission as mystic itinerary."[16] Today it is the sense of God as *mystery*, beyond human concepts and formulations, rooted in the personal experience of faith, that characterizes the search for God, for the hidden God of our age. Face to face with the radical challenges to Christian mission, the bearers of the Gospel in the midst of any society—of other faiths or of unbelief—must speak from an authentic experience of God, personal or within community, or it will fail to gain a hearing. This experience must arise today and in the decades to come, as it has always arisen, from a living out of the Paschal Mystery in one's own life—in prayer and contemplation, in the labors of witnessing to the Gospel, in discernment in the Spirit, in the fundamental dedication to and involvement with the poor, the suffering, the broken, and the powerless in this world—"to the uttermost limits of loving" (John 13:1). This has always been the authentic way of Christian mission; in the end, there is no other way.

The work of mission is finally the work of the Spirit of God.[17] In the 1990s, as in the past, we will seek to discern both the signs of the times and the ways by which we must respond to them. But in all this we must seek to be obedient to the Spirit, for in that obedience alone can we second God's renewing of the face of the earth.

Notes

1. "Mission in the 1990s: I. Arthur F. Glasser and II. Michael Amaladoss," *International Bulletin of Missionary Research* 13, no. 1 (January 1989). The present contribution should really be considered only a postscript to Fr. Amaladoss's more comprehensive treatment of the theme. Cf. also his book, *Mission Today* (Rome: Centrum Ignatianum Spiritualitatis, 1988).

2. Cf. *For All the Peoples of Asia, Vol. I: The Church in Asia: Asian Bishops' Statement on Mission, Community and Ministry, 1970–1983* (Manila: International Mission Congress, 1984) and *Vol. II: Further Texts, 1974–1986* (Manila, 1987). Also, Guadencio B. Rosales et al., eds., *Toward a New Age in Mission: International Congress on Mission, 2–7 December 1979, Books I–III*, 2 vols. (Manila: International Mission Congress, 1981).

3. E.g., for India: Felix Wilfred, *The Emergent Church in a New India* (Tiruchirappalli, 1988), and for the Philippines, Brendan Lovett, *On Earth as in Heaven: Corresponding to God in Philippine Context* (Quezon City, Philippines: Claretian, 1988). See also Lovett's *Life Before Death: Inculturating Hope* (Quezon City, Philippines, Claretian, 1986).

4. Words included within quotation marks are taken from FABC texts, but especially from the "Final Statement of the International Congress on Mission, Manila, 2–7 1979." Cf. n. 2, above.

5. FABC papers, Joseph A. Komonchak, *Towards a Theology of the Local Church* (Hong Kong: FABC Secretary General's Office, 1986). The Theological Advisory Commission (TAC) of the FABC intends to issue its study-paper on the theology of the local church in the Asian context in the spring of 1990.

6. Cf. Niall O'Brien, *Revolution from the Heart* (New York: Oxford University Press, 1987), a remarkable account of base ecclesial communities (BECs) in the diocese of Bacolod, Negros island, Philippines, which deserves an even wider audience than it has already reached.

7. Cf. the "Final Statement of the IMC, Manila, 1979." See n. 2, above.

8. Cf. Arthur Glasser, in the article in *International Bulletin* cited above in n. 1.

9. "Evangelization in Asia Today," Statement of the FABC All-Asian Conference on Evangelization, Suwon, South Korea, 24–31 August 1988. FABC Office of Evangelization, Shillong, India, 1988, no. 6. FABC Papers, no. 50, *The Urgency of Christian Mission* (Hong Kong: FABC Secretariat, 1988), pp. 74–78.

10. Cf. part 3: Agenda for Future Planning, Study and Research in Mission, from the Research Seminar on the Future of Mission, March 8–19, 1981. Rome, Italy. Mary Motte and Joseph Lang, eds., *Mission in Dialogue* (Maryknoll, N.Y. Orbis, 1982), pp. 633–49. Also James Scherer, "Roman Catholic Mission Theology: The Impact of Vatican II," *Gospel, Church and Kingdom: Comparative Studies in World Mission Theology* (Minneapolis: Augsburg, 1987), esp. pp. 196–232.

11. John Wijngaards, "New Ways for Mission," in *Tablet* (London), 22 October 1988, pp. 1208–9. Recent and stimulating, on the implementation of these principles and policies, is Vincent J. Donovan, *The Church in the Midst of Creation* (Maryknoll, N.Y.: Orbis, 1989). Cf. also Walbert Bühlmann, *The Church of the Future: A Model for the Year 2001* (Slough, England: St. Paul, 1988).

12. Joseph A. Komonchak's "field theory" on the self-realization of the local church deserves attention. (Cf. n. 5, above.) Some lucid and helpful pages will be found in Severino Dianich, *Chiesa Estroversa. Una ricerca sulla svolta dell'ecclesiologia contemporanea* (Torino: Edizione Paoline, 1987), esp. pp. 110–22, and in Michael Amaladoss, *Mission Today* (cf. n. 1, above), pp. 164–66, from which the quotation is taken.

13. Niall O'Brien's book, cited in n. 6, above, spells out the revolution of hope that the base ecclesial communities can awaken.

14. On diverse realizations of community, see "The Church as a Community of Faith," FABC Papers no. 29, 1982, p. 15. On Pope John Paul II and "solidarity," cf. his encyclical *Sollicitudo Rei Socialis* for the twentieth anniversary of *Populorum Progressio*, 30 December 1987, Vatican City, 1987.

15. Pope Paul VI, *Evangelii Nuntiandi*, on evangelization of the world in our time, United States Catholic Conference, Washington, D.C., 1975.

16. Pierre Schouver, *L'Église et la Mission, Croire et comprendre* (Paris: Centurion, 1977), pp. 140–42. Cited in *Toward a New Age in Mission* (cf. n. 2, above), vol. 1, book 2, pp. 152–53.

17. See Lesslie Newbigin, *Mission in Christ's Way: Bible Studies* (Geneva, World Council of Churches, 1988).

Holistic Mission from an Orthodox Perspective

WCC Photo: Peter Williams

Bishop Anastasios

Mission will always remain the central ecclesiastical matter; an expression of the life and vitality of the church. Unthinkable as it is to have a church without liturgical life, it would be even more unthinkable to have a church without missionary life.

Secularization in a Changing World

The complex and changing world within which the church is called to live out its mission needs to be studied continuously and thoroughly so that the march, language, and meaning of the contemporary world may be understood. The 1990s will find humanity moving with accelerated speed toward greater interdependence, while the environment continues to be violated and destroyed. At the same time, we will see astonishing discoveries in space, in biotechnology, and in genetic reconstructions. And we must expect further surprises on the social field. Recent events in socialist Eastern Europe announce clearly the coming radical changes.

Questions about the mystery of the world and the essence of humankind become more and more pressing. An intense pluralism and a tendency toward relativism influence philosophical and religious thought. In this century there has been an enormous numerical increase of those who call themselves atheists and agnostics. This community of disbelief is exceeded today only by the Christian and Muslim worlds.

The religious quest has not lost its force and continues to define the life of many societies. But in the developed countries religion has withdrawn to the sphere of the individual. For mis-

Bishop Anastasios (Yannoulatos) of Androussa is Professor of the History of Religions at the University of Athens, Acting Archbishop of the Orthodox Church in East Africa, Moderator of the Commission on World Mission and Evangelism of the World Council of Churches, and Editor of the missionary review Panta ta Ethni.

sion in the 1990s, the big problem remains secularization. Our duty is to pursue loving dialogical contact with our fellow men and women, many of whom every day walk with us without identifying with either the believing community or the antireligious community.

Given the crucial problem of "faith and science" in our secularized world, a living Eastern Orthodox theology could bring to bear some distinct characteristics; for example, a personalistic, existential theology that culminates in a theology of the divine energies. Accentuating the significance of the person and the divine initiative on behalf of the world, Orthodox theology can open new ways for Christian dialogue with the modern sciences. Our endeavor is neither a fatalistic submission to contemporary technological culture nor a sterile negation of it. Rather, it is how we can, in a climate of apocalyptic concerns, work for the renewal and transformation of culture.

The Electronic Age: A Third Period of World History

In the first stage of civilization, human beings summarized their origins through oral traditions, myths, laws, and institutions. Later, the written word led to a second level utilizing the oral

---

For mission in the 1990s, the big problem remains secularization.

---

tradition and pushing it forward into space and time. During the past few decades, we have entered a third period of world history. We proceed at great speed in the electronic world, which, combining oral and written word with visual media, offers us unimaginable flexibility, range, and speed. These new possibilities not only make human thinking more agile and fluid, but also give new dimensions, inclinations, and powers to human intelligence.

The Christian message that was carried in the vessels of the oral and written word in the former centuries must now be conveyed in a timely and correct way. It has to be tuned with the dynamics of the new media that mold the common sense and the universal human conscience. On this level we have remained behind in our theological education as well as in our ecclesiastical practice. Have we been taken by surprise? Are we slow to move because of our traditional character and way of thinking? There is need of serious reconsideration concerning the education of priests, missionaries, and other workers of the church in order to make full use of the new possibilities offered by the new era for the transmission of the Gospel.

The Emergence of a New Europe

The most important new situation in the 1990s is undoubtedly the rapid and radical changes in the socialistic countries of Eastern Europe and the emergence of a new Europe. These societies, after a long, painful experience of the communist system, are searching for a new direction and orientation. It is not true that their dream is capitalism. Of course their longing is freedom and creativity, but the ideals of a just, peaceful society remain predominant. What type of democracy will emerge? What insights will inspire it? The new generation receives not only the good inspirations of freedom but also faces the invasion of the dangerous products of Western secularized culture.

The church has the opportunity to play a decisive role, offering the message of Christ who gives priority to love. The missiological implications are enormous. We must have the courage for a self–criticism and proper estimation of the mistakes and shortcomings made during a previous phase of the history of these peoples, when church and state were identified and the church's leadership accepted a high-society style of life and thinking.

Since many of the churches present in the transforming socialist countries are Orthodox, I feel obliged to say that we must avoid beautifying the Orthodox past in every detail. Many aspects require serious revision and repentance. Sensitivity for the social process; participation in the building of a free and just society through prophetic witnessing, service and consequent life in Christ; intellectual capacity and wisdom to deal with new scientific discoveries and challenges; courage to say the truth before the authorities; and readiness to accept martyrdom, remain serious principles for Christian mission and evangelism.

But also among Christians a deeper understanding is needed. When the snow that covers a country has melted, then the different colors and gaps—suspicions, controversies, and even enmities—may appear again. Especially the temptation of various Protestant groups to proselytize among the Orthodox people can emerge, creating problems and damage. Recently 10,000 copies of the Bible were sent from abroad to a small number of families (less than twenty!) of a Romanian Orthodox congregation. In this Romanian version of the Bible the word ''idol'' has been consistently translated as ''icon'', thereby undermining the Orthodox Christians who during all these years of communism through resistance and suffering kept the Christian church alive in this country.

The development that takes place in the Soviet Union will have, sooner or later, an influence upon other socialist countries, and also upon China. Communism has played a role of bulldozer, destroying many old traditional structures. Are Christians ready to tackle the values, longing and dreams of the young generation, and offer the right orientation in the post-communist period that is emerging?

Finally it is expected that all these social changes will have an effect in the Third World. New challenges and opportunities are before us and need a creative and prophetic presence of the Christians around the world.

Religious and Cultural Multiformity

Although we must take full account of the coming technical culture, we should not forget the traditional way that survives in many societies, in all continents: old cultures, traditional structures, states of mind, conditions of life. However powerful the currents that push humanity toward a world community with common characteristics, the religious and cultural multiformity of the world will remain intense.

In the past two decades the discussion of the theological significance of other religious beliefs has gone on with increasing tension in certain theological circles, which has caused serious uneasiness. Western Christian thought comes often to a polarization: Some people deny the worth of religious conceptions outside the Bible; others question the uniqueness of Christ.

For the Orthodox Church, Christ is the incomparably great and absolute One. Hence, there is no need to diminish others in order to exalt his magnificence. His greatness, always revealed in the mystery of humility and love, does not despise anyone or anything, but shows the truth that exists even in the most simple inspiration within the history of the world.

In an analogous way, our living experience of Christ and our longing to be united with him do not awaken any enmity toward others but give us freedom from preconceived ''views'' and ''fears.'' Christ imparts an infinite love that, like a strong magnet, discovers even the tiniest particle of love that exists among the array of religious ideas, shapes, and symbols. It collects them with respect and doxological disposition and rejoices at the mystcal light that penetrates through the most dark folds of human history in personal and universal fields.

This in no way means compromising the Christian Gospel. Our message cannot cease to have as its center an event: "God was manifested in the flesh, vindicated in the Spirit" (1 Tim. 3:16). He who was incarnated, crucified, and resurrected, the Lord who is to come again in order to recapitulate all things, remains to all ages the axis of our preaching. Mission is an inner necessity for the faithful and for the church. If we deny it, we not only refuse an obligation, we deny ourselves.

Wholeness of the Church's Experience and Message

Being faithful to God, we are obliged to obey the fullness of the divine will, the whole of the Gospel and not just half of it. Since ancient times, in the Orthodox Church this call was heard: "Make us worthy to do your will not half way, but to fulfill all, as you will" (St. John Chrysostom). This holistic view and approach demands that we assume all the truths of revelation, that we be faithful and consistent in following all the commandments of the Gospel, and that we contemplate the whole mysterious plan of salvation. We proclaim him "who is, and who was, and who is to come." We are not preoccupied with the past only. The catholicity and wholeness of the church's experience defines this vision.

Faithful to the catholicity of the Christian tradition, we have to remember in missionary quests and efforts the trinitarian, cosmological, eucharistic, and eschatological dimensions of the faith. Individual and communal life, personal sanctification and social justice, local cultures and openness toward a world community, are within the ecclesiastical interest of the church.

The faithful live with "a burning heart for the sake of the whole creation," according to the expression of Isaac the Syrian (Sermon 81). The whole cosmos has been called to participate in the restoration that has been achieved through the incarnation, the redeeming sacrifice, the resurrection and ascension of Christ. In Christ, God has assumed human nature entirely and by that, the whole creation. Our concern is a longing for the unity of all things. All things are to be reconciled through and in Christ, finding their relationship to the Logos of God (Eph. 1:10). In this process the church, that is, the body of Christ in space and time, has a central role: to serve the universal unity in a cosmic dimension.

Growing into Unity

Division in the Christian church continues to be the great scandal of humanity and a terrible restraint for world mission. Every effort, labor, and struggle for the mutual rapprochement of Christians acquires a special missionary meaning and value.

Growing toward unity is not only a deep human desire but also a hopeful vision echoing the express will of Christ, voiced at the beginning of his Passion: "That they all may be one . . . , so that the world may believe that thou hast sent me." In this prayer, we do not see only the deep concern for unity of his disciples, but also the basis, the root of this unity—"that they may be one *in us.*" The unity for which we are asking cannot be rooted in a ground other than in the "in us" emphasized by our Lord.

We have to grow toward unity in different levels of our own Christian commitment, starting from the parishes, dioceses, local churches, where so often cracks and divisions occur. We have also to extend our concern to wider circles in national and ecumenical levels. There is a two-way traffic. The more we contribute with prayer, love, and humility to the coming together of those who long for God, the more we approach Christ, the center of the universal unity. And on the other side, the more we are struggling to liberate ourselves from our small ego (personal or

There is no need to diminish others in order to exalt the magnificence of Christ.

collective), having him as a guide in all the details of our life, our desires, thoughts, and actions, being in a deep communion with him, the more we grow into an essential and deep fellowship and unity with all human beings.

The Radiating Power of the Saints

The church radiates the gospel of salvation mainly as a *communion of saints.* Within the church militant, the saints known and unknown contribute in a mystical way to the world mission. This is done through prayer, the spiritual mobilization they create by their own existence. Many saints circulate among us, endowed with love and grace, self-denial and humility, forbearance, patience, and spiritual power. According to tradition, God sent Saint Anthony the Great to Alexandria to meet a shoe-repairer who had reached spiritual heights as an ascetic. The church has never lacked those unknown shoe-repairers throughout the twenty centuries of its life. They contribute to the quiet and convincing transmission of the Gospel. We sometimes hear of heroic women, largely unknown by the world around them, who have struggled their whole lives in the midst of poverty; with self-denial they have brought up their children, having always on their lips the phrase "Glory be to you, O God." Thus they contribute to the promotion of the Gospel message. Our church is not merely the theories, the schisms, the theological disputes, but the unknown pages of the lives of the saints who live the Gospel faithfully.

The Local Church Participating in the Sufferings and Expectations of the World

As the holy, catholic, and apostolic church in a certain locality,

each community of the faithful must participate in the suffering and struggles of the whole church throughout the world. Each ecclesial community participates in the universality of the church. Surely, a local church presents distinctive features, and it is by these distinctives that it is called to glorify God and give its witness. At the same time, it is a primary requirement for every diocese and parish to experience the universality as well as the locality of the church.

Each local church, in order to be genuinely catholic, must pray for and be ready to serve in the most destitute regions, where people are starving for the word of God, where the Christian presence does not exist or is imperceptible. In this way the church remains faithful to its apostolicity and catholicity.

Stressing the fact that every country is a place of mission, including one's homeland, is undoubtedly correct. But the view that there is no more need for "external mission," that the local church is solely responsible for its own region, is dangerous. When a local church or parish is absorbed by its own concerns, spiritual withering results. To close and isolate oneself is to lose oneself. This is a spiritual law that is valid for the life of individuals, the community, and smaller and larger entities.

Mission: A Celebration of Joy

It is time to intone the Gospel as an overflowing of thanksgiving and joy, for the unexpected gifts of God, his love "which passes all understanding," and the light, hope, and fullness of life brought by his resurrection. This deep experience of joy and hope, which pulsates within the heart of the faithful, cannot be kept within the narrow limits of oneself. It radiates from us, and thereby thanksgiving to the Father is expressed more directly and existentially. The central sacrament of the church, the Divine Liturgy, which recapitulates and doxologically summarizes the church's faith, is a "Eucharist," a "Thanksgiving," a thankfulness that is experienced in celebration. The strongest wine is the wine of the Divine Eucharist, which intoxicates us with unselfish love, with a sober joy that no one and nothing can take away from us (John 16:22).

Drawing constantly from the well of inspiration and power found in the Divine Eucharist, mission becomes a doxological movement, declaring the final hope for the future of humanity and the whole universe and an invitation to feast in it. The radiation of this essential joy, full of hope, a joy that quietly overcomes sin, suffering, and disdain, has been from the beginning the characteristic of a genuine Christian community. It is only with joy, the joy of unselfish love, the joy of the permanent presence of the resurrected Christ, with this feast of the Resurrection, that the church proceeds victorious in the world. And if she were to lose this joy, she would also lose the world.

Acting in Local Context with a Universal-Eschatological Perspective

In the World Mission and Evangelism Conference that took place in San Antonio, Texas, May 1989, with the theme "Your Will Be Done—Mission in Christ's Way," the two most important trends were the spirit of catholicity and the passionate will for the fullness of the Gospel. The central idea of the conference was defined as the need to discern the will of God in local conditions, while preserving the sense of the wider plan of God within history. Some months later, in August 1989, during the meeting of the

Central Committee of the World Council of Churches in Moscow, this decisive contribution of San Antonio was again affirmed.

Between the two gatherings, the "Manila Manifesto" was drafted and approved by evangelicals meeting in the Second Lausanne Congress (Manila, July 1989). The manifesto and the congress itself, with the theme "Proclaim Christ Until He Comes," moved in a similar direction.

This convergence of thoughts, realized within the period of four months by conferences covering the whole spectrum of the Christian world, is very significant indeed. These meetings took place in cities belonging to the so-called first, second, and third worlds: San Antonio in the technologically developed West, Moscow representing the Eastern socialist countries, and Manila representing the developing world of the South.

It is this synthesis of universal perspective and realistic sensitivity in confronting local needs and the challenge to act in the local context, while keeping a universal perspective, that will define the missionary effort in the last decade of the twentieth century.

Fifteen Changes for Tomorrow's Mission

Ralph D. Winter

Change is the password of the 1990s—changes in perspective, changes in concepts of task and goal, and changes in methodology.

Changes in Perspective

1. New Missions from Former "Mission Fields." The existence of thriving "national" churches in the so-called mission lands is no longer the only "great new fact of our time." As we plunge into the 1990s, not just church life, but possibly an even more important indigenous, national *mission movement* is springing up from within those countries that were once "mission fields."

Of course, there never was anything really new about a church on the mission field, because the process of expanding across cultural frontiers began as soon as there were two or three gathered together in the name of Christ outside the Jewish cultural tradition. Neither is there anything essentially new about mission-field Christians becoming missionaries in their own right. The Western world itself is merely a mission field that has become a mission sending base. And it is well known that most of the South Pacific was missionized by South Pacific islanders themselves, learning foreign languages and going from island to island extending the Christian movement.

But now there are over fifty indigenous mission agencies that are members of the India Missions Association. The Asia Missions Association is nearing its twentieth year of existence. At the global level the Third World Missions Association is picking up momentum. In Nigeria, there is not only a strong association of Nigerian mission agencies, but one member mission alone is sending over six hundred missionaries to untouched language

---

Ralph D. Winter was a Presbyterian missionary in Guatemala from 1956 to 1966. He then taught on the faculty of Fuller Theological Seminary School of World Mission for a decade before founding the United States Center for World Mission in Pasadena, California, of which he is the Director.

groups in and outside of Nigeria.

What will be truly new in the 1990s is the astounding prominence and vastly larger muscle of the "third world" mission movement. It will possibly overtake Western missions, in terms of total number of missionaries, by 1995 (Pate, 1989:45–46).

Thus, the crucial and still-unreached goal is no longer merely the growing unity of a global church movement but the strategic interfacing of a *global mission movement*.

2. Triumphalism vs. Fatalism. In the past we have seen both of these extremes. But it is to be devoutly hoped that during the 1990s the Lausanne Statistics Task Force, or some other serious body, can bring into widespread public view a far superior picture than most people now have of the true status of the growth of Christianity in comparison to other world religions. Surely there must be some remedy to wild quotations like "Muslims are growing at 16 percent and Hindus at 12 percent while Christians are only growing at 9 percent. I have heard this precise phrase from the lips of three different prominent church leaders, but am entirely at a loss as to where such outlandish numbers came from. What is indisputable is that population growth rates (apart from immigration) range from 0.6 percent per year in Germany to slightly over 3 percent for Egypt. But the *vital* sector of the Christian

---

The third world mission movement will possibly overtake Western missions, in terms of total number of missionaries, by 1995.

---

sphere, which already numbers in the hundreds of millions, is growing by more than 6 percent, and *there is no other religious or political bloc of comparable size with an even remotely comparable growth rate.*

During the third of a century when it was easy to assume that everything had gone wrong in China, some theologians developed a theology that excused us from concern over the growth rate of Christianity. However, the adverse comparisons in the quotation up above, besides being untrue, unnecessarily undermine the entire Christian world mission.

3. The Sending Culture vs. the Receiving Culture. The 1990s will not likely improve greatly the ability of the general citizenry in a sending country to see themselves as those from other countries see them. Yet nothing is more obvious and embarrassing to those of us who have lived in a foreign country for any length of time than the tendency of our people back home to take the worst of the other country and compare it with the best of our own, the sending country. That is no way to see ourselves as we really are!

Americans rail against poor populations overseas supporting themselves by supplying the American appetite for drugs, while not wanting to acknowledge the onerous drug trade that Western governments have perpetrated for more than a hundred years. Are we Americans overlooking our gigantic international cigarette market, which is not only subsidized in this country but with the help of our federal government is literally forced upon certain Southeast Asian nations by political processes attempting to "protect" our own drug growers? Panama's government is not the only one that has been involved in pushing drugs. What if

our exports to Thailand prompted their troops to invade North Carolina and burn the tobacco plantations—the source of our enforced export of that highly addictive drug. What if they circled the White House, seized the president, and flew him off for trial in Bangkok?

Do we realize we have a hundred times as many alcoholics as hard drug addicts? Will we send troops to smash our own distilleries or to Scotland to take care of their export whisky production?

How do we look to foreign eyes when we get more violent about a Central American dictator who sasses us than we do about an East African dictator who is determined to starve 4.5 million human beings who are "the wrong tribe"?

We are told that certain Japanese government publications warn against and caricature certain foreign visitors. These documents are surely as outrageous as they are outlandish. But, unfortunately, we can find the same desperate provincialities in our own country wherever people are as isolated from personal contact with foreigners as most Japanese are. Probably no one force in world history has done more to reduce these kinds of phobias than the activities of the Christian world mission. But the 1990s are much too short for any great change to take place—except within the Christian movement itself.

Changes in Concepts of Task and Purpose

4. The Nature of the Task. One of the most urgent areas of reflection and transition, even at this late date in history, is in the area of understanding the basic task of the Christian world mission. In the 1980s great progress was made in recognizing the wholeness of the Gospel. This is reinforced by new understanding of the full meaning of the word *blessing* as it occurs in the Genesis version of the Great Commission, namely Gen. 12:1–3; 18:18; 22:18 (Abraham); 26:4, 5 (Isaac); and 28:14 (Jacob-Israel). One nation is *blessed,* and all nations are to *be blessed.* What does this mean? Tony Campolo tells us that it does *not* mean finally being able to afford a BMW!

In English the word *blessing* implies merely a *benefit*—not also a *relationship,* as in the Hebrew *barak.* Americans—even American missionaries—typically do not understand the full significance of the privileges, obligations, and permanent benefits of the *family relationship.* Yet a relationship of just this significance *is* implied in the Hebrew *barak.* The implications here are profound and exceed the normal intent of evangelistic appeals. For example, in a family relationship you do not choose between evangelism and social action.

Will the 1990s bring us closer to the full meaning and implications of making into one family people from every tribe and tongue and people? Is the hymn still ahead of most of us: "Who serves my Father as a son is surely kin to me" (Oxenham, 1913)?

5. The True Receptivity of World Religions. This century has emphasized anthropological insights about cultural relativism, and many missionaries today are strikingly better equipped to understand the strong and weak points of all human cultures. But it is still possible for us to reject entire religiocultural systems *en toto.* We have semantic "snarl" words such as *syncretism* and *accommodation* for anything tainted with foreign religion. Yet it is precisely in the area of religion, and specifically in the quest for the best words for *God,* that we may have our most significant points of contact with other religious systems.

How can we believe, on the one hand, that all humankind

derives from God's creative handiwork and, on the other hand, expect in our mission contacts to find none of that handiwork still remaining? Why need we quibble about the use of the word *Allah* for *God*? Arabic-speaking Christians for centuries before Mohammed prayed to *Allah*. The New Testament itself employs a deeply deficient term for *God* in the Greek *theos*. Only centuries later, for English speakers, the word *God*, despite its pagan origin, was adapted and newly charged with meaning.

Phil Parshall's recent book, *The Cross and the Crescent*, goes in the right direction. Will the 1990s allow us to realize that some of the most *devout* Muslims are closer to the kingdom than (1) shaky Muslims who are apparently coming our way only due to their rejection of their own faith or (2) purely "culture Christians" who don't really believe and obey anything? Isn't the Islamic cultural tradition—prayers, mosque, and entire way of life—far more redeemable than the ancient hellenic way of life with which Paul was willing to work?

6. The Myth of Closed Countries. In the 1990s this never-correct concept will hopefully be broken down almost completely. It is fueled by those who have certain specialized mission services to offer. It has been a favorite theme for those who stress "tent-making" or who are in the Bible-smuggling business, but it tends to paint an unrealistic picture that undermines obedience to the Great Commission. This emphasis may not only divert monies from worthy agencies that are doing unpublishable work in "closed countries," but it may also reduce the guilt level of those who do not in any event wish to support the Christian world mission.

7. The Number of Unreached Peoples. Many missiologists agree that the most strategic goal to aim for is establishing a viable, indigenous, evangelizing church movement within every human culture, that is, *within every community sufficiently homogeneous to enable all to hear and understand in their own milieu.* Where such an internal witness is lacking, such groups are defined (by a widely representative Lausanne-sponsored meeting in March 1982), as "Unreached Peoples." It is inevitable that this number can

---

The Bible does speak of every group being at least partially represented in the ultimate family of God.

---

only be *estimated* until all clusters of such groups are actually penetrated and the necessary homogeneity is confirmed.

This is so crucial a goal, and is so foundational to mission, that I have thought it justified to coin a term for the basic concept behind this March 1982 definition. I have suggested the term *unimax* peoples, since, as defined, the concept involves the *max*imum sized groups still sufficiently *uni*fied to allow "the spread of a church planting movement without encountering barriers of understanding or acceptance."

Careful compilations of two or three thousand groups already exist. These compilations, according to the March 1982 definition (1) list some Unreached Peoples (*unimax* peoples) more than once if their people are found in more than one country, (2) often list as a single group what are actually *clusters* of unreached *unimax* groups but at least (3) include virtually all remaining unreached

unimax groups within these clusters. Nevertheless, it is fairly safe to say that once church-planting efforts take place in these clusters, these lists of groups will turn out not to include many more than twelve thousand total Unreached Peoples by the March 1982 definition. The Lausanne Statistics Task Force has agreed on twelve thousand as a reasonable estimate of the number of these relatively small people groups that are still unreached. Even as we enter the 1990s, the task of making new missionary penetrations into twelve thousand new cultures is being parcelled out to the various sectors of the mission sending base all over the world—continent by continent, country by country, and even denomination by denomination.

Thus, all of this lays down one of the most concrete and significant mandates for the 1990s: reach all such (unimax) groups by A.D. 2000. Or, to use more precise language: establish by the year 2000 *a viable, indigenous evangelizing church movement within every people that is the largest group within which the Gospel can spread by a church-planting movement without encountering barriers of understanding or acceptance.*

8. The Challenge of the Cities. The astonishing thing is that once the definition of Unreached Peoples is clear, it is possible to anticipate that the global urbanization of humanity may very soon carry at least a few key individuals from every *unimax* people into a city somewhere in the world, where they will likely be much easier to reach. In the 1990s the gradual urbanization of much of the world will continue, and it may well be that by the end of the 1990s a slight majority of the world's population will be found in cities. The continuing existence of nationalities and ethnic groups in the cities, and even the creation within cities of new groups, will require us to be much more perceptive about the different kinds of peoples we need to deal with in the growing cities of the world.

9. The Concepts of Closure and Countdown. One of the expectable and irrepressible trends in the 1990s—at least until the middle of the decade—will be for many to do what was done a hundred years ago, namely, to try to answer the essentially unanswerable question, "What will it take to complete the Great Commission, and can it be done by the year 2000?" Those who feel it is necessary to wipe away every tear, resolve every social problem, and cure all poverty, disease, and injustice may not be attracted to schemes to conclude the task by the end of the century. However, the Unreached Peoples terms make realistic, I believe, the year-2000 goal of completing the necessary initial missionary penetration of every unimax group. This is a heartening and strengthening challenge to work toward with all we have to give. This goal is essentially a refined version of the one developed at the Edinburgh 1980 World Consultation on Frontier Missions: *A Church for Every People by the Year 2000.*

Meanwhile, many other goals are being forged for completion by the year 2000. Some of them are not, strictly speaking, *closure* goals, that is, they do not *complete* any particular process but simply constitute legitimate, measurable goals to shoot for. An example would be the goal of planting a million churches by the year 2000. By contrast, DAWN's closure version of this goal aims to plant a church in *every* "small group of every class, kind and condition of people in [each] country" by the year 2000, however many that may be—an estimated total of 7 million new congregations (Montgomery, 1989: 18, 53). Incidentally, by my calculations, this additional 7 million churches would only about double the present number of *vital* congregations worldwide.

Some Roman Catholic mission leaders have set another significant goal, for which no closure version exists: enough individuals being won to the faith that half of the world's population will call itself Christian by the year 2000. I personally think it is best, however, not to think in terms of conquest—*how many are won* to the faith—but of extending opportunity: *how many have been given a chance to respond.* The Bible seems to give no basis for assuming that any particular percentage of the world's population will become Christian on a personal level. Rather, the Bible does speak (mysteriously) of ethnic groups being "discipled" in some sense, which is clearly not a case of winning either a certain number of persons or of winning a certain percentage. To plant "a viable, indigenous, evangelizing church movement" (a paraphrase of the 1982 definition) only requires some minimum, vital, incarnational response within a group. Yet the Bible does speak of *every* group being at least partially represented in the ultimate family of God.

Changes in Methodology

10. *The Free Expression of Worship.* Already it is obvious that the world church is rapidly taking on the cultural characteristics of the so-called pentecostal-charismatic tradition. This shift is being resisted, but mainly by nongrowing groups. Our modern world is now irretrievably more of an emotion-accepting world. It is no longer only at football games that the full range of human emotions can be expressed.

This is not to say that emotions are now being invented or created or that the Christian movement had no emotional content before. It is certainly not as though the Spirit of God has been out of action all these centuries. Rather, there is a new dimension in what is increasingly a world *mood*, which has allowed Christian groups in recent years to give this element legitimate public expression. It would not appear that the 1990s will retreat in this area.

11. *Recovering from a Professionally Trained Ministry.* Despite the normal perspective of new missionaries sent out from the United States, the Christian movement on a global level continues doggedly to depend upon informal apprenticeship methods of ministerial training rather than the historically recent adoption in the United States of a European state-church style of professional education in residential schools. This is mainly because apprenticeship is more versatile and flexible than the classroom. It may even be that movements in the United States, such as the rapid growth of the new charismatic congregations often called "Christian Centers," will assist the Christian movement to outgrow the kind of professional processes of ministerial formation that have been so assiduously cultivated in the past fifty years in the United States. The fact is that wherever seminaries—or other types of lengthy residential programs—have been introduced overseas and *made mandatory for ordination,* the growth of the church has been severely crippled.

Thus, what has in some circles become almost universally hailed as a legitimate goal—a seminary education—may become more clearly a questionable goal in the 1990s, even in the United States. It is hoped that the goal of a highly trained ministry will be retained, but methods other than an extractive, residential process will be employed. The latter must be seen both as an inappropriate technology for most of the world, and also as an undesirable method even where it is employed. The Assemblies of God now has its own seminary in the United States, although its great strength was achieved without the help of this kind of

residential training that generally tends to exclude older persons, as well as those with jobs and families.

12. *Going to, through and beyond Partnership.* In the 1990s we will increasingly come to doubt the universal applicability of the very idea of *partnership in mission.* We arrived at the concept legitimately as missionary efforts produced church movements around the globe. Wherever those efforts succeeded, it became necessary to shift gears from *outreach* among untouched populations to church-to-church *relations,* and the definition of *mission* has adjusted to fit.

Westerners tend to think in terms of *political entities* and to mistake them for *nations* in the ethnolinguistic sense. Many of our church boards have overlooked until recently the fact that in most countries they are dealing exclusively with, or through, one tiny minority population and are therefore unable to deal fairly and effectively with the many other legitimate peoples and nations of that same country.

If Christianity were only today reaching the United States through Japanese missionaries to the Navajo Indians, the logic of *partnership in mission* might suggest that the resulting Navajo

> ## Dealing with one church per country started as an administrative convenience, but has turned out to be a missiological nightmare.

church be called "The Church in the United States." This could happen even though, say, its membership were entirely within the Navajo nation. Worse still, it might then be expected that all other Americans could best be reached only through Japanese partnership with Navajo Christians. Worst of all it might imply that the Navajoes could not reach out on their own without the Japanese being involved. The worst thing, ultimately, is when *partnership* has been employed to deny the validity of any pioneer evangelism at all—because a church must already be there to be able to invite missionaries!

Thus, what for Western mission offices has been an administrative convenience (dealing with one church per country) has turned out to be a missiological nightmare. Missiologically, it would be far better to denote church movements by their culture base than their country. However, surging national churches in the 1990s will drastically question the significance of the partnership perspective on a country-wide basis.

13. *Pluralistic Church, Plural Mission.* Pluralism in mission is one of the inevitable developments in all the older church traditions, especially those that have over the centuries expanded into strikingly different parts of the world or within the highly pluralistic United States. A wholesome pluralism is the natural outgrowth of an intelligent response to rich diversity. But a pluriform unity in a sending church cannot easily be expressed through a single office. In fact, a pluralism in mission fully expressing the pluralism of the home church is a goal yet to be achieved for most Protestant denominations as we begin the 1990s.

United Methodists have sprouted a new unofficial mission

board in Atlanta, which is opposed by Methodist leadership just as the Church Missionary Society was opposed for many decades by the Anglican hierarchy. The Roman Catholic tradition has provided us with many excellent models to demonstrate that mission orders are *in order* in Protestantism. The Internal Revenue Service in the United States is currently involved in a study of what the Protestant equivalent of a Catholic order would look like.

14. Home and Foreign Boards. In the shuffle of recent history, many church boards have wondered if the old home/foreign dichotomy is valid. It is easy to put all mission in a single board, as some denominations have done, but this may only perpetuate a confusion about the very definition of mission.

It is hoped that in the 1990s, the fact that thousands of Unreached Peoples have at least some small representation within the United States will be recognized as requiring classical foreign mission work to be pursued at home. But local churches and donors are not prepared for this and deny funding to those eager to take strategic advantage of the opportunities here. Mission money tends instead to go only to those who have been willing to go and "suffer" in foreign circumstances. Thus support for missions builds on sympathy for the *missionary* rather than concern for the *mission purposes* involved.

This faulty prioritization is not something that will quickly be resolved, even though its grievous deficiencies are eminently clear. *Frontier mission* work everywhere in the world needs to be cut out of cloth different—both in training and approach—from the kind of mission that emphasizes helping churches to expand within their own ethnic nationalities but that does not necessarily help them to reach out to Unreached Peoples beyond them. The fact is that the vast majority of missionaries is involved in existing church programs; at most, 15 percent of all missionary personnel is engaged in expanding the boundaries of opportunity for the Gospel.

15. Value in Secular Approaches. Dozens of major mission agencies, both denominational boards and interdenominational agencies, have seen fit to found secular entities through which they can offer valid, understandable services without confusing governments with their religious terminology. This method of approach has proven to be helpful and will continue to increase.

Bibliography

Montgomery, Jim. *DAWN 2000: 7 Million Churches to Go.* Pasadena Calif.: William Carey Library, 1989.

Pate, Larry D. *From Every People.* Monrovia, Calif.: MARC Publications, 1989.

The Poor: Starting Point for Mission

Mary Motte, F.M.M.

As we enter the final decade of the twentieth century we are obliged to write a new missiology. A gradual evolution over the past twenty-five years has reached a level of demarcation with past understandings. The starting point for mission now begins with the poor of the earth. Their different realities in popular movements networking for solidarity and community throughout the world are shaping mission for the years ahead. Base ecclesial communities, part of this larger phenomenon, are specifically affecting understandings of mission. In addition, one must also take into consideration the religious awareness of various kinds present among the poor, especially their sense of sacredness in creation.

Vatican II awakened a fresh exploration of the church's relation to the poor, a relation rich in tradition but somewhat ambiguous in recent centuries. Change became more emphatic when the Latin American bishops met in Medellín in 1968 and interpreted Vatican II for the Latin American continent principally as a preferential option for the poor. Their reflections guiding this decision were situated in a larger historical context in which the poor had begun to take in hand their destiny through various grass-roots liberation movements. This option shifted the focus of mission to a new place, namely, the place of the poor, not only for Latin America but eventually for the whole world. The call to all persons to hear the Gospel message comes from their place.[1] Some twenty-two years later, a significant proportion of theological studies, papal encyclicals, documents from episcopal conferences, and decisions by missionary institutes reflect a preferential

Mary Motte, a Sister of the Franciscan Missionaries of Mary (F.M.M.), is Director of the Mission Resource Center of the F.M.M. in North Providence, Rhode Island. She is Research Consultant to the United States Catholic Mission Association and Roman Catholic Consultant to the Commission on World Mission and Evangelism of the World Council of Churches.

option for the poor. If mission is to be a credible Gospel witness, then it must begin with the experience of the poor.

This does not mean that mission is something that is brought into the lives of the poor, but that the place of the poor is where the reign of God is always on the way of coming to fulfillment. Anyone who would be concerned about mission must start there, discovering first of all what God is doing.

Discerning mission issues for the 1990s involves consideration of the experience of the poor, the consequences of a preferential option for the poor, and the new parameters for understanding mission.

The Experience of the Poor

When the Latin American bishops referred to the poor, they meant those who lack basic necessities and for whom daily life is a struggle. This same understanding attaches to various theological reflections concerning the poor. The reason for this perspective is that these people exist in the most critical space of creation, at the juncture of conflict between good and evil. It is the space where structural sinfulness builds up forces of oppression and violence that deprive the poor of their human dignity.

To recognize such structural evil is not to deny the presence

---

If mission is to be a credible Gospel witness, it must begin with the experience of the poor.

---

of personal sinfulness. Even while the poor are those who offer us the starting point for mission, they are also in need of conversion. But the issue of conversion cannot be addressed apart from that of structural sin. Striving for survival very often causes interpersonal relationships to break down, and the immediate consequences can hide the real sources of systemic oppression and violence that make survival so difficult. Oppression and violence tend to stifle humanness in the poor.

As poverty increases on a world scale, more and more people are caught in situations of violence and oppression. At the same time, a growing number of popular movements among the poor are indicative of their increasing awareness that they must retrieve their dignity through mutual collaboration with others who share the same condition. Those who once were forced to vie with one another for the crumbs from the tables of the rich are now discovering their own power in mutuality and collaboration.

Base ecclesial communities, a specific type of popular movement among the poor, are of particular interest in a consideration of mission issues for the 1990s, because formation of these communities around the Word of God provides a model for understanding the dynamism at the heart of mission. Vatican II described mission as the responsibility of every baptized person and essential for the life of the church. *Evangelii Nuntiandi* illustrated the importance of this insight when it spoke of the community gathered around the Word of God being transformed for mission. The base ecclesial communities especially exemplify this understanding of mission, and for this reason it is helpful to consider the elements that constitute the structure of these communities:

1. the poor gather as disciples in memory of Jesus, celebrated in Word and Sacrament;
2. they read the Word of God in the context of their history, recognizing that God is alive and present with them;
3. conversion begins within the community encountering the Word of God;
4. the poor begin mutually to trust one another and form bonds of communion through their shared experience of God's love in their lives;
5. they seek to share this experience with the larger society.

In other words, mission involves an experience of God calling a community to conversion and sending it forth with the message of love. It involves a mutuality of commitment among community members to read the Word of God and celebrate it sacramentally, responsive to the conversion this calls forth from each member. From this experience the message is brought to those who have not heard.

Boff speaks of these communities as a new birth in the church. They bear witness to God's mission of bringing creation to fulfillment, that is already present in the interaction between the Word of God present in history and the community allowing that Word to enter its life. In this way the church becomes the sign of God's salvific will for all persons.[2]

A Preferential Option for the Poor

The experience of base ecclesial communities and a preferential option for the poor expressed by leadership with responsibility for the service of universal mission are interrelated, not causally but as two developments that took place in the same historical context of the past quarter century. Both had their origins in Latin America and as such do not necessarily represent a model to be copied by the rest of the world. Nevertheless, they do indicate a new model of evangelization understood as a calling to awareness of the meaning of the Gospel message for our times. In these years the Roman Catholic Church has become a world church. The unity of the Gospel lived in a plurality of ways is developing new expressions of faith in Jesus Christ and of ecclesial unity around the Bishop of Rome.

Development of a preferential option for the poor can be traced most consistently for our purposes by looking at the missionary institutes and societies that are at the service of universal mission. Traditionally, these have been sisters, brothers, and priests and remain so to a great extent. However, growing numbers of laity are being called to this service in the Roman Catholic Church. At present, a number of them are attached in some way to the missionary institutes, and therefore share in the visions and orientations these groups have developed.

Just about all of the missionary institutes in one way or another have taken a preferential option for the poor. This choice has led them to examine their activities and question their decisions. Traditionally, the members of these groups have made a vow of poverty or have had some form of commitment to live simply. Institutionally, they have not been poor but have had material resources provided out of their own sharing and contributions from others to carry on mission. They have examined their use of resources and determined how to put these more effectively at the service of the poor. Greater simplicity in lifestyle has been actively promoted, with an emphasis on smaller communities or living groups that have to grapple with day-to-day existence in ways not experienced in larger institutional facilities. Formation of new members and continuing education of other members has led to a probing examination of what an option for the poor means in concrete attitudes, methods, and choices in mission.

There was little immediate experience to build on from within the institutes, but two sources provided insight: (1) a return to the original sources of inspiration for their foundations, which were often poor, small, and simple; and (2) the growing experiences of the base ecclesial communities of the poor. These became foundational criteria for interpreting what an option for the poor meant.

A study including the results of a survey of Roman Catholic missionaries conducted by the United States Catholic Mission Association (USCMA) provides concrete data on what this option has led to among its member missionaries.[3] The critical areas being examined are the context and focus of the missionaries' work; the concerns of the people among whom they are working; and the missionaries' understanding of missionary proclamation. Information given about contexts in which the missionaries are located, and concerns of the people, show that practically all of the missionaries are working in situations of extreme poverty and oppression. The greatest concerns of the people are most often for the basic necessities of life, such as food, clothing, shelter, and work. The fact that the missionaries are in these situations would appear to reflect a preferential option for the poor, predicated on social analysis determining where the poor are who are truly on the periphery of society.

After social analysis, insertion is the next step in the process of articulating an option for the poor. Those who are called to the service of universal mission are at the service of the reality of the poor, and therefore insertion is a logical consequence. This means being with and walking in solidarity with the poor. And one does not just do this overnight; it is a journey into the world of the poor that begins with an invitation from those who are poor to join in their struggle and reality. For that invitation to be issued, one has first of all to be present to the reality of the poor: simple presence that is ready to receive and that stands before the other with respect and empty hands. It is a contemplative stance that recognizes the God who became incarnate, took upon himself human suffering, and who is present.

> There was no history of church; people had to form new relationships; learn to live with people of different tribal traditions . . . much of my time is spent being with, listening to, searching together for some answers to the questions that life here poses . . . the desert is hostile . . . there are none of the usual tribal ties that bind, root and unite people here . . . everyone is relocated. Our main focus is to help one another survive, and to help build the relationships we need if we are going to survive here . . . then beyond survival . . . together to build our "family" here, our community, our church.[4]

The person at the service of universal mission, that is, the missionary, carries a message of hope, the good news of God's love for each person. The call to universal mission is a call to be at the service of the poor. The essence of this call is an experience of the love of God for each person that knows no limitation. God loves each one in a unique, concrete, existential way as evidenced in the Incarnation. The call to universal mission is a call to embody this message of good news especially for those who are least likely to hear it because of the conditions in which they live, for example,

the poorest, the oppressed, those who live on the periphery of society. A missionary in Korea notes:

> I work in labor apostolate—a new special work that tries to bring the church into contact with lower paid workers and link with farmers' groups and city poor by trying to bring the church's social teaching to modern day Korea that it may be a sign of concern for the workers and a sign of hope for all.[5]

Other missionaries describe their understanding of proclamation as follows:

> To be the hope, the joy, give people a glimpse of God, which they need in order to survive.

> To live so fully the mystery of life that people know without a doubt God is present in our lives even in the doubts and mystery . . . to share life so fully with our neighbors that we explain to each other the Gospel of Jesus.

> To be living witnesses of the Gospel of Jesus by sharing the life of the people among whom we work.

> [A] presence bearing witness; trying to hear God speak to us and then proclaiming the values of His Kingdom in the line of the prophets. It means challenging and being challenged, i.e., called to constant conversion of the individual and social structures.

> My understanding of proclamation is that every thought, word, feeling and action of mine should proclaim the Word Who has come to liberate the captives and bring in a new Jerusalem where all can live in brotherhood/sisterhood, in peace, justice and love.

> [C]alling forth to the fullness of life as revealed in Jesus Christ.[6]

In summary, various experiences of missionaries illustrate that a preferential option for the poor is a choice made by those called to the service of universal mission and involves: social analysis of situations to determine where the poor are; insertion

---

The call to universal mission is a call to embody the message of good news especially for those least likely to hear it.

---

into the situation of the poor; an attitude of respect and listening, being present to; awareness of the hope in the message of good news that one bears in a personal experience of God's love.

The Parameters of Mission

Mission that starts with the experience of the poor has three concerns: human dignity, relationships, and community. Its ultimate goal is the fullness of God's reign. Practically all of the missionaries who responded to the USCMA study questionnaire are inserted in places that lack essential resources for a life imaging the dignity of the human person. Injustices rooted in economic, racial, sexist, religious, and/or political factors are the causes of these situations. People experience deep poverty and cruel oppression.

Chart Your Course for the Decade of Destiny, 1990-2000

David Barrett and Todd Johnson, previous authors of books in the "AD 2000" series, draw on the most advanced and comprehensive missions data base available anywhere to provide readers with a fresh look at the global evangelization movement.

As we approach the year AD 2000 our world is changing faster than ever before. The pressures are intensifying—and the doors of opportunity are opening wider for Christian witness. Will you be prepared?

OUR GLOBE AND HOW TO REACH IT

Seeing the world evangelized by AD 2000 and Beyond

by David B. Barrett and Todd M. Johnson

GLOBAL EVANGELIZATION MOVEMENT

The AD 2000 SERIES

Using facts, diagrams, and the authors' research, *Our Globe and How to Reach It* offers authoritative and clear answers to vital questions such as:

How far have we come in taking the gospel to the whole world? or What would the world look like if it were evangelized by the year AD 2000?

In addition, *Our Globe and How to Reach It* provides:

- 33 one-page global diagrams which uncover the past, describe the present, and explore future possibilities in world mission.
- A quick reference guide to global Christian statistics allowing you to find any fact within seconds.
- A list of 200 global goals describing how major Christian denominations and agencies plan to reach the world for Christ by the year AD 2000.
- A checklist of 109 steps Christians can take now to make the nineties a real Decade of Stewardship in world evangelization.

Whether you are a church leader, missions executive, professor of evangelization, or a concerned Christian layperson, *Our Globe and How to Reach It* will give you the hard data you need to set your course for the nineties.

OUR GLOBE AND HOW TO REACH IT by David Barrett and Todd Johnson—0-936625-92-9, $6.95

Previous releases in the AD 2000 Series include:

COUNTDOWN TO 1900 by Todd M. Johnson—0-936625-69-4, $5.95

700 PLANS TO EVANGELIZE THE WORLD by David B. Barrett and James W. Reapsome—0-936625-55-4, $6.95

COSMOS, CHAOS, AND GOSPEL, A CHRONOLOGY OF WORLD EVANGELIZATION FROM CREATION TO NEW CREATION by David B. Barrett—0-936625-18-X, $5.95

EVANGELIZE! A HISTORY OF THE CONCEPT FROM B.C.420 TO A.D.1987 byDavid B. Barrett—0-936625-17-1, $5.95

WORLD-CLASS CITIES AND WORLD EVANGELIZATION by David B. Barrett—0-936625-00-7, $5.95

WORLD IN VIEW by Keith Parks—0-936625-08-2, $5.95

UNREACHED PEOPLES: CLARIFYING THE TASK by David B. Barrett and Harley C. Schreck—0-912552-58-1, $5.95

New Hope
P. O. Box 12065
Birmingham, AL 35202-2065
(205) 991-4933

GLOBAL EVANGELIZATION MOVEMENT

The AD 2000 SERIES

It is not easy to enter into the lives of the poor, but unless one enters their lives, one cannot engage in a dialogue that will articulate the message of the good news of God's love. It is by entering into the situation of the poor that the person at the service of universal mission shares in a dialogue communicating good news. Each instance of such a dialogue replicates that begun in the Incarnation, when God in Jesus Christ humbly entered the human condition, and began a conversation expressed in human love and caring, a service of washing another's feet.

Engagement in such dialogue begins to restore the experience of dignity robbed from the poor by violence and oppression. Human dignity is the most basic need of the poor who are caught in situations of oppression and violence. In the measure that dignity is gradually restored for the poor, the poor begin to assume responsibility for their lives. Liberation through Jesus Christ is incarnated in human reality. Those at the service of universal mission do not bring liberation; rather they bring a message of hope as part of a dialogue. The partner in dialogue is the Spirit of God present among the people, often in new and different ways.

Broken relationships are common in the experience of the poor. Without dignity they are often not able to enter into relationships that endure or reinforce a sense of bondedness. As mentioned earlier, their situation often places them in a condition of vying with one another for favors from the rich and powerful. They try to survive, and that can become a very personal agenda.

Building mutual trust toward more stable relationships is another aspect of the dialogue between the poor and the missionary. The first step in such an effort is to reflect together on the living Word of God present in their midst, how God is acting in their lives. As insights are shared, and hopes begin to be spoken and entrusted to one another, relationships begin to grow, and community is formed. As community bonds grow, the poor can begin to address those conditions that have deprived them of their dignity, and they can begin to liberate themselves from what has oppressed them.

The major focus of the missionaries' efforts is concern for human dignity, relationships, and the building of community in various situations of insertion among the poor. The goal of this commitment is to communicate how much God loves each person now, and how this will be fully realized in the time of God's reign announced in Jesus Christ. It is important to note that the model for the missionaries' efforts is found in the base ecclesial communities of the poor, in which the community gathers around the Word of God and is transformed by this experience. Therefore, the model for missionaries at the service of universal mission is found first of all among the Christian communities of the poor. They have articulated the dynamism of mission, that is, the transforming, liberating relation between community and God's Word.

Those called to the service of universal mission have a particular responsibility to make it possible for this liberating, transforming relationship to occur in those places where there has been no prior effective communication about the love of God. It is in such places that the efforts to focus on human dignity, relationships, and community become more clearly the service of universal mission. God's love knows no bounds, and no one is excluded. Therefore, the persons who are called to universal mission are at the service of the poor in all situations. The poor do not have to be Christian, and it need not be the intention of the missionary to make them so. The first call is to be present, to stand before and recognize how God loves them, and then to gradually enter into a dialogue that will articulate that love in the bondedness of human community. God's love is without condition, and those who are at the service of universal mission cannot place conditions on any dialogue that wishes to communicate something about that love.

Conclusion

At the beginning of this article I noted the need for a new missiology that starts with the experience of the poor. The most striking occurrence in that experience is the growth of popular movements of the poor networking around the world. Communal bonding predicated on human dignity and positive interpersonal relations are the elements in these movements that describe most accurately what is happening. The significance of these elements becomes clearer in the examination of what happens in the base ecclesial communities, where these phenomena are brought into the Christian experience. Liberation from oppression and suffering can be seen more clearly in their essential relation to salvation in Jesus Christ and the coming reign of God.

Mission begins in this place of the poor, in the building up of community. Theologically, the life of the Trinity as a model of communion is the basis for all community. It is the model of the reign of God and therefore the missiological model directed to the realization of the reign. Missionaries at the service of universal mission are called to situate themselves at the service of the poor. They have no agenda to accomplish but simply to approach the poor with respect, bearing only their own experience of God's love. A dialogue that begins with listening and discovering the Spirit of God among the people is the way of mission. Proclamation is an experience of God that spills over and at the same time grows through the experience of others, even those outside the Christian experience. It is concerned with everyday life as intimately related to the experience of liberating grace.

At the beginning of the last decade of the twentieth century, members of missionary institutes, whether lay, religious, or clerical, are persons at the service of universal mission. They are bearers of one part of a dialogue that speaks of God's love and wills that all be saved. Their task, if one can use that word appropriately, is to be at the service of the poor and to discover in their midst their partners in dialogue. This requires a deep personal experience of God and a humble openness to discover God's presence in ways not expected. It involves the pain of rediscovering human dignity in the midst of oppression and violence. Mission is all that leads ultimately to the experience of community focused on the reign of God. The symbol and sacrament of this experience is the community of disciples gathered in the memory of Jesus, celebrating his presence in Word and Sacrament and continually being transformed.

Notes

1. Cf. Joseph Gremillion, ed., *The Gospel of Peace and Justice: Catholic Social Teaching since Pope John* (Maryknoll: Orbis Books, 1976); Gustavo Gutierrez, *The Power of the Poor in History* (Maryknoll: Orbis Books, 1983). A. Hennelly, *Liberation Theology: A Documentary History* (Maryknoll: Orbis Books, 1990).
2. *Ecclesiogenesis* (Maryknoll: Orbis Books, 1986).
3. United States Catholic Mission Association (USCMA) Research Project, unpublished report, 1990.
4. USCMA data.
5. USCMA data.
6. USCMA data.

Live and Learn at the
Overseas Ministries Study Center

Fully furnished
apartments at
moderate rates are
ready for you to
move in. Write for
current Study
Program Schedule
and Application
for Residence.

Since 1922 OMSC has welcomed into residence more
than 8,000 missionaries and overseas national church
leaders. We invite you to join us, sharing your experiences
and gaining fresh insight into the challenge of world mission.
Choose from a wide variety of weekly seminars to aid
spiritual renewal and sharpen cross-cultural skills.

Those wishing to earn the OMSC Certificate of Mission
Studies do so by participating in fourteen or more of the
seminars offered and writing an evaluative paper at the
conclusion of their residence at OMSC. Senior Scholars
in Residence offer supportive fellowship and assistance
with mission study projects. OMSC provides an interdenominational, international, and interdisciplinary
learning atmosphere.

 **OMSC**

Overseas Ministries Study Center
Gerald H. Anderson, Director
490 Prospect Street
New Haven, Connecticut 06511
Tel: (203) 624-6672

The "Old, Old Story" and Contemporary Crises

WCC Photo: Peter Williams

Emilio Castro

In June 1989 the World Council of Churches Commission on World Mission and Evangelism held a conference in San Antonio, Texas, to address mission in the 1990s under the title "Your Will Be Done—Mission in Christ's Way." For a full discussion of our topic, I refer the reader to the report and publications from that conference. Here I limit myself to three emphases that I consider central to authentic mission today.

Telling the Story of Jesus

Mission in the 1990s needs to concentrate on spreading the actual knowledge of the story of Jesus of Nazareth. "Tell me the old, old story" is the refrain of an old hymn we used to sing in Sunday School. Yet the telling of that story is our most urgent mission challenge today. We are confronted by secular societies, by a spreading consumerism in which even the central aspects of our faith like the incarnation of the Son of God have been transformed into objects of commercialization. Jesus, the church, Christianity, are taken for granted. Especially in the Western world churches belong to the panorama, but not many people expect important things to happen through them: "Can anything good come out of Nazareth?" (John 1:46). Once again the answer to our modern world needs to be: "Come and see." The passing of the Christian tradition, the events of the life of Jesus Christ, to the present and coming generations is both fundamental and difficult: fundamental, because finally it is the only contribution we have to offer to modernity—a mirror, a point of reference, a yardstick, a life, Jesus Christ; but difficult, because this very life has been made the object of manipulation and reductionism, of soap operas, of commercial deformations. In the jungle of competitive offerings of miracle solutions to all human problems, a finger pointing clearly to Jesus, the Lamb of God, is the best service we can render to the world today.

It is easier to see the fundamental importance of this central dimension of our missionary work when we consider present events in former socialist societies, where the breaking down of a monolithic culture built around atheistic presuppositions is opening doors for the recovering of religious experience and religious participation. But the real danger is that this religiosity that eagerly looks back to old national traditions is not necessarily recovering *the* tradition of Jesus Christ. The growth of alliances of ethnic groups and confessional affirmations, whether in Yugoslavia or the Ukraine, etc., indicates the highly sensitive situation confronted by the churches. On the one side they are called to occupy the spiritual vacuum left by the disappearance of a prevailing ideology and are invited to fulfill their classical roles of preserving loyalty to and integration of society. On the other side, that appeal to the churches is not always made on gospel grounds but as a convenient tool to provide cohesion in societies that are searching again for their historical identity. The real challenge is to put gospel content to the new church loyalty, to provide a direct link to the story, teaching, life, death and

> **A finger pointing clearly to Jesus, the Lamb of God, is the best service we can render.**

resurrection of Jesus Christ as the foundation stone on which to rebuild personal and social life.

The emotion of religiosity is there but the knowledge is lacking. The translation, publication, and distribution of the Bible are once again central to the fulfillment of our vocation. Countries that have been fighting for years for permission to print or import limited numbers of Bibles (where even today, on the black market, a Bible is sold at astronomical prices) are in desperate need of gospel literature that can provide real-life content to the religious symbols. After so many decades of being denied education with Christian references, there is an accumulated challenge to provide those references for the older generation and to assure especially that today's children and teenagers know the sources of our Christian faith so that they may have valid points of reference to go beyond their ethnic loyalties to loyalty to the Savior, Redeemer, and Lord of all.

Another aspect of our present situation that obliges us to concentrate our thoughts on the telling of the story of Jesus Christ is interreligious dialogue, which is an increasingly common experience for Christians in every corner of the earth. The interreligious encounter that in the past was the privilege of missionaries or travelers is becoming today an experience available to every Christian. It is important in these encounters to be aware of the nature of our distinctiveness, of our contribution, and of the center of our life. The story of Jesus Christ is the real novelty, the new breakthrough. In the 1990s, like the apostle Paul, we must be ready to say: "For I decided to know nothing among you except Jesus Christ and him crucified" (1 Cor. 2:2).

Emilio Castro, a Methodist minister from Uruguay, is General Secretary of the World Council of Churches.

The Redeeming of History

Mission in the 1990s needs to recover afresh Jesus' way of mission. The year 1992 is an obvious reference date; five hundred years have passed since the Spanish arrived in America. Official celebrations will be organized in Spain and every main city in Latin America. For Spain it is a clear attempt to remind the world that their country was a great power, that there was a time when the sun never set over the Spanish empire. But for the church of Jesus Christ it is also a reminder of the fact that along with the conquerors came the missionaries, and the Gospel was spread all over the continent. The strange historical alliance of the sword and cross has meant the submission of practically all inhabitants of the continent to the Roman Catholic Church. It is a model of evangelization that belongs to our history, with its shadows but also with its lights. The question for us is not to engage in a celebration of that colonial past nor to profit from that occasion to celebrate the fact that Protestant missions came to Latin America to break the cultural monopoly the Catholic church had enjoyed in this continent during so many centuries. It is not a moment for the glorification of the past; it is a moment for a sober assessment of its meaning, especially from the perspective of the indigenous Indian population or the black people who were brought as slave laborers to this continent.

From a European perspective a Te Deum could be called for: from the perspective of the oppressed people of the Americas, the survivors of the original inhabitants of those countries, it will be the occasion for a Requiem. We cannot change history; we can only try to redeem it. The fact is that the church of Jesus Christ is planted in the Americas. The Spanish conquest is a historical fact. Whether we want it or not, there is no way back, but there is a way forward in the spirit of Jesus Christ to claim the best of the Afro-American heritage and see how that heritage illuminates our perceptions and our obedience to Jesus Christ. Can we, out of the treasures of the Gospel, come afresh to recognize the hidden and permanent richness of the Indo-African culture and religiosity? The Americas were not an empty continent. Diverse and multiple developments of great civilizations flourished there among the Incan, Mayan and Aztecan peoples. Great advances had been made in agriculture, food production, social protection of the poor, etc. There was no freedom in the Americas, just as there was no freedom in Europe either at that time. But the replacing of Incan power by the conquerors' power was not at all linked to the Gospel of Jesus Christ but to the thirst for gold, wealth and power. Now the moment has come to reclaim the best of the Gospel of Jesus Christ, which was brought to the Americas in the earthen vessels of the institutional church.

The attempts developed by liberation theology to read the Gospel afresh from the perspectives of the poor in Latin America are good and needed beginnings. Notwithstanding internal church debates around that theology, the fundamental challenge of our mission—to allow the poor people of the continent to be bearers of God's mission—is clearly established.

But 1992 and the years beyond will open a new chapter in European history. The disappearance of the Berlin wall is symbolic of the disappearance of traditional barriers all over Europe. The constitution of the European Economic Community as a single market and eventually as a confederation of European states brings challenging questions concerning the identity of the European continent. Societies built upon an atheist philosophy are coming close to collapse, and it is evident that churches and religious movements will play a much more important role in the new societies. This is a chance for the whole of Europe to raise basic questions on the aims of their living together, the values for their community life.

A proposal is being advanced from inside Christian circles to shape Europe as a Christian continent; a serious missiological debate is necessary to discuss alternatives. Personally, I do not believe that it would be good for the total mission of the church in the world if a particular region were considered a "Christian continent." That would invite other religions to constitute a fortress of their own and would also mean an invitation to Christian minorities in other continents to emigrate to Europe, the so-called Christian continent! One of the major difficulties of Christian minorities, especially in Asia, is precisely that of their recognition as full citizens of nations where the majority of the population and sometimes the public institutions recognize other religious loyalties. "Mission in Christ's Way" will invite us to think of Europe not as a Christian fortress but as a place where Christians are able to proclaim the Gospel of Jesus Christ as full participants in all sectors of society, so that the spirit of Jesus Christ may permeate that society.

It is very difficult for Christians in Europe to avoid a certain

> **The vision of God's triumph makes it impossible to look for sanctuary in quietism, neutrality, or withdrawal.**

sense of triumphalism as they see the developments in Eastern Europe and the incredible economic developments of the West! Should they not dream of returning to the values of an "ideal" Christendom of the Middle Ages? The Reformation took place and the value of a personal decision before God was duly emphasized. The American and French revolutions took place demanding the full freedom of the person and accepting religiously pluralist societies. The Marxist revolution also took place and dimensions of social justice belong today to everybody's consciousness. There is no way back but there is always a way forward in the spirit of Jesus Christ. It is in interaction with all those forces that have shaped the life of humanity, especially in Europe in the last four or five centuries, that a new Europe will be rebuilt. Inside that rebuilding we need to formulate the Gospel of Jesus Christ and our Christian vocation. Maybe the answers provided by liberal Christianity to the challenges of modernity were inadequate, but their awareness of the challenges and the attempt to cope with them in a humble, servant, dialogical witness and spirit are of fundamental importance for today.

"Mission in Christ's Way," in Christ's spirit, with Christ's attitude, is central to our acceptance of the plurality of religious opinion prevailing in the world today. Our challenge is to build societies where peoples of different religious loyalties will live side by side, giving testimony to their respective convictions and uniting forces in the building up of a common society. In the last decades we took for granted that a secular society of Western style was the model that could provide religious freedom and tolerance everywhere in the world. Today we discover that especially our Muslim friends are unable to accept a secular society because this contradicts some of the Qur'an's fundamental affirmations concerning the rights of God over all human life. Christians who are proclaiming the Lordship of Jesus Christ could also be tempted by a theocratic organization of society; however, since that Lordship is the Lordship of the crucified Christ, this temptation should be resisted.

The challenge before us is how to help shape societies able to recognize common human values that could be supported from different theological and philosophical perspectives—in particular, how to provide for living together in full religious freedom within a frame of reference that recognizes the significance of the spiritual values cherished by great sectors of the population. Having recognized that Western secularism is a philosophical approach that is not neutral, we have embarked on a common search for new styles of conviviality, with more respect for the faith affirmations of the diverse sectors of society. Indonesia found a tentative agreement with the famous Pancasila ideology. Countries like Nigeria and Sudan are dramatically searching for an answer to this dilemma. We all will learn from their sufferings!

A Christian mission carrying on the model of powerlessness of Jesus Christ will be able to participate humbly in the search for models of society that would allow the free expression of our respective convictions.

The Renewing of Creation

Mission in the 1990s will need to be mission in the power and wisdom of the Spirit. As we learn to think of the future, two different phenomena call the World Council of Churches to concentrate on a prayerful search for the presence and action of the Holy Spirit. One is the new power acquired by humankind to manipulate life in such a way as to question seriously the notions of the spirit, of freedom, and of responsibility. We have here, of course, serious ethical problems and socioeconomic consequences, but more important are the implicit challenges to the whole humanistic tradition of the Christian faith that has affirmed human freedom, the capacity to respond to God's calling, and the dialogical nature of human beings as an affirmation of the image of God in humankind. The mission of the church will be obliged to spell out the meaning of spirituality in a world in which all aspects of life have been brought under the control of scientific, almost mechanistic styles of work. In this theological and spiritual research we might be assisted by new affirmations of modern science about the fundamentally chaotic, arbitrary, perhaps even freedom-filled reality, which seems to consitute both the micro- and macro-systems of the universe. Interaction between that prevailing chaos and the human capacity to perceive an organized reality is the new intellectual battleground against which the perception of the spiritual world, the presence of God, the reality of prayer, the calling to repentance and conversion, and the affirmation of the infinite value of every human being needs to be affirmed and tested.

This is a theological, intellectual challenge of first magnitude. The powerful reality of the spiritual life in the poor people of the earth, the reality of the growth of the church through charismatic renewal should be an encouragement to theological work that fully assumes the responsibility of challenging the lack of spiritual references, of transcendental dimensions in so much of the contemporary intellectual debate. When it is announced that we will put a person on Mars in the year 2020, when new technologies are developed to penetrate the mysteries of the creation of the universe, we need to hear again the simplicity of the Psalmist who said: "When I look at thy heavens, the work of thy fingers, the moon and the stars which thou hast established; what is man that thou art mindful of him, and the son of man that thou dost care for him?" (Ps. 8:3-4). From this understanding we have the capacity today to respond intellectually, ethically, and existentially that human beings are creatures made by God's hands, called to develop relations with God, relations of love, freedom, and communion that go far beyond whatever could be measured or weighed.

There is a new growing awareness of the world of nature, as created and sustained by God, which challenges easy dismissal of the earth as only a tool or a material at the disposal and arbitrariness of human beings. The ecological catastrophe that threatens the world today demands, of course, technical responses, but much more is needed: a fundamental repentance for the total disregard and exploitation of nature for the benefit of humankind that should open up to a new awareness of God's love for the whole of reality. The Spirit, like a mother, hovering over the initial chaos, is God's Spirit caring for the creation even today. Psalm 104:30 is the basic biblical reference for the 1991

> **Ecological catastrophe demands a fundamental repentance and a new awareness of God's love for the whole of reality.**

Assembly of the World Council of Churches: "When thou sendest forth thy Spirit, they are created; and thou renewest the face of the ground."

This renewal for which we pray should be a powerful component of our missionary proclamation today. But the concentration on the Spirit is called for also by the manifestation in the life of the church and the emergence of new Christian communities and movements that claim a new awareness, a new presence of the Holy Spirit. Inside the ambiguities of history, with all the manifestation of human frailty, this is a fact which is calling our attention. Diverse manifestations of renewal are taking place within the churches, and millions of poor people proclaim the wonders of new life and new communities through the manifestation of the Spirit. Our response to these movements needs to be one of thankfulness, of analysis, and of participation in the common search for a total spiritual renewal of the Christian church. We are very much aware of the fact that one of the gifts of the Spirit referred to in 1 Corinthians 12:10 is the capacity to discern, to tell the difference between gifts coming from the Spirit and those that are not. When praying for the gift of the Spirit we venture with hope and expectation of an encounter with Christians who today confess gladly the wonders of the manifestations of the Holy Spirit.

Conclusion

The mission of the church should concentrate especially on spreading the actual knowledge of the life, death, and resurrec-

WE'RE A ONE-CLASSROOM SCHOOL!

One thing is certain today: if you're going to make a difference for Christ, you need a school whose classroom is the world. One that will help you minister to people of vastly different cultures.

That's why you need to consider the School of Intercultural Studies at Biola University. SICS will give you the tools vital to the success of your ministry in any cultural setting. We'll also help you understand what America will be like in the next generation as part of a world that's growing smaller each day.

With a full range of degree offerings,

SICS has the program you need. All of our faculty members hold the highest degree in their field—and they bring to the classroom over *100 years* of combined service in international mission!

SICS is committed to helping you develop a program geared to your experience and goals, with creative project work and participation in the school's teaching and research activities.

We can help you

chart your course in a world where the old lines are being erased. To find out more about the School of Intercultural Studies at Biola University, write or call today.

1-800-OK-BIOLA toll free
In CA 1-800-99-BIOLA

Detach and mail this coupon.

I want to learn more about the School of Intercultural Studies.

☐ Please send me information about the programs available at the School of Intercultural Studies at Biola University.
☐ Please send me information on financial aid.

My Name _____
Address _____
City _____ State _____ Zip _____
Phone (____) _____
Expected term of entry: ☐ Fall ☐ Spring 19____
Major or graduate program _____
Degree now held _____
Graduate of _____ Year _____

Mail to:

BIOLA UNIVERSITY
ADMISSIONS OFFICE • 13800 BIOLA AVENUE • LA MIRADA, CA 90639

Toward a New Paradigm of Mission

tion of Jesus Christ. This is the foundation stone for the rebuilding of personal and social life. In the spirit of Jesus Christ we need to look at our history critically and to assess both the manifestations of God's grace and of human sinfulness; in that way we will be able to redeem history and to proclaim today a fresh appreciation for God's gifts to every nation, to every people, and with the treasure of those gifts invite all nations to the banquet of the kingdom, to the celebration of the Lamb of God. We need to look also to the future with a mission that will contribute to the creation of human societies in which the main common values of humanity will be preserved. The testimony we render to the Gospel of Jesus Christ will be our basic contribution to the shaping of those new societies of tolerance, conviviality, and solidarity.

Finally, as we look to the future, we are invited to pray, "Come, Holy Spirit—Renew the Whole Creation," because it is only in the power of the Spirit that we will be able to confront both the intellectual and existential challenges of today: intellectual, in the sense of preserving, affirming the image of God in every human creature and discerning God's concern for the totality of the creation; existential, in participating in the historical struggles to overcome personal and social evil, and to plant signs of the kingdom. The mission of tomorrow needs to be aware of the wonders that the Spirit is achieving already today so that we open wide the windows of our lives and the windows of our churches to the inbreaking of the freedom of the Spirit of God.

WCC Photo: Peter Williams

David J. Bosch

A New Paradigm

Crystal-gazing remains a hazardous undertaking. What is mission going to look like in the 1990s and beyond? Perhaps more important: what *should* mission look like?

In some circles there are signs of what Max Warren—shortly before his death in 1977—referred to as a "failure of nerve." Even in those circles where people proceed as if mission means "business as usual," there seems to be, deep down, nagging questions about the nature and content of the missionary enterprise. Can we simply continue to interpret mission as telling the "old, old story"? How do we remain faithful both to the faith delivered to us and the unprecedented challenges facing us?

What we are facing today in mission is, however, by no means the first major crisis that has confronted the church. It has faced similar crises in the past, e.g., when it felt forced by the logic of Jesus' ministry to move beyond the confines of the people of the "old" covenant, or when, in the seventeenth and eighteenth centuries, the Enlightenment tore asunder the centuries-old unity of religion and culture, faith and life. And now—at least since the end of World War II—we are facing a crisis at least as pervasive as those earlier ones. It is this circumstance that has led to widespread uncertainty and even malaise. Still, as Hendrik Kraemer said more than thirty years ago,[1] this does not mean that we stand at the end of mission; rather, "we stand at the definite end of a specific period or era of mission, and the clearer we see this and accept this with all our heart, the better." We are called to a new "pioneer task which will be more demanding and less romantic than the heroic deeds of the past missionary era."

David J. Bosch *is Professor and Head of the Department of Missiology in the Faculty of Theology at the University of South Africa, Pretoria, and Editor of* Missionalia, *journal of the Southern African Missiological Society.*

During the past few years I have been struggling to articulate (first for myself, but then also, perhaps, so as to help others) the nature and implications of six major challenges the Christian missionary movement has had to face during the past twenty centuries. The outcome is a manuscript that will be published in 1991 by Orbis Books under the title *Transforming Mission*. Drawing on Thomas Kuhn and Hans Küng,[2] I suggest that in the past each major crisis has led to a "paradigm shift" in missionary thinking and praxis. My purpose is to trace the contours of a new paradigm of mission now emerging as a response to contemporary developments. Out of a total of thirteen elements in the new paradigm, I want to discuss here just three: contextualization, common witness, and eschatology.

Mission as Contextualization

It seems to me that one of the major "discoveries" of recent decades—a discovery that has far-reaching implications for our understanding and practice of mission—is that every living theology is by nature a *contextual* theology. Early Christians sensed that the Gospel had to have meaning within the context of a particular situation, and they theologized accordingly. Our four Gospels are, to no small degree, four different attempts at con-

---

The Gospel is foreign to every culture and inculturation is never a completed process.

---

textualizing the Gospel for different situations and readers. In the subsequent centuries, however, the Christian community began to lose sight of the intrinsically contextual nature of the Christian faith. Ideas and principles were deemed to be primary, eternal, and unchanging; their "application" was merely secondary. Deviations from what was held to be "orthodox" were declared to be "heterodox"; creeds were designed to encapsulate the "eternal truth" and were used as shibboleths to determine the difference between acceptable and unacceptable views. This pattern persisted for many centuries in all branches of Christianity.

A breakthrough came only recently, with the discovery that not only was all theology contextual but also that this was the only way in which theology can be meaningful. J. L. Segundo expressed the new "epistemological break" as taking the form of a "hermeneutical circle" in which praxis has the primacy and reflection becomes a second (not a *secondary*) act of theology.[3] Thought is not to be conceived as prior to being, nor reason to action; rather, they stand and fall together.

Contextualization means the end of any universal theology and suggests the experimental and contingent nature of all theology. This does not mean that the context is to be taken as the sole authority for theological reflection. In fact, where this happens, we do not have contextualization, but *contextualism* (where "God" is reduced to and identified with the historical process).

The rediscovery of the contextual nature of all theology has had particular importance for what has become known as "liberation theology" in all its forms. At least since the time of Constantine, theology was conducted "from above" as an elitist

enterprise (except in the case of minority Christian communities, traditionally referred to as "sects"); its main source (apart from Scripture and tradition) was *philosophy*, and its main interlocutor was the *educated nonbeliever*. Contextual theology, on the other hand, is theology "from below"; its main source (apart from Scripture and tradition) is the *social sciences*, and its main interlocutors are the *poor* and the *culturally marginalized*.[4]

If the theme of *liberation* constitutes the first and best-known model of contextual theology in our own time, then the theme of *inculturation* represents a second important model. The Christian church was born in a cross-cultural milieu and, in the early centuries, inculturated itself in a variety of societies: Syriac, Greek, Roman, Coptic, Armenian, Ethiopian, etc. After Constantine, however, the church itself became the bearer of culture and put its peculiar Western stamp on the Gospel. Blind to the fact that its theology was culturally conditioned, the Western church in modern times exported its assumed supra-cultural and universally valid theology with little compunction to the non-Western world. In order to expedite the conversion process, however, some adjustments had to be made. In Catholic missions this strategy was usually called "accommodation" or "adaptation"; in Protestantism it was referred to as "indigenization." These terms were, of course, not applied to the church in the West: there the faith was already fully "at home." What had long ago been completed in the West had, however, still to take place in the Third World.

The exigencies of the accommodation debate are well known, particularly as they emerged around the so-called "Rites Controversy" in China and India. After that, the terms of accommodation were rigidly circumscribed in Catholicism. In Protestantism the situation was only apparently but not really fundamentally different. Protestant mission agencies pursued the ideal of the "Three-Selfs" for "their" younger churches: the latter were expected to become self-governing, self-supporting, and self-expanding churches. A fourth "self," self-theologizing, is only now being added. For a long time any form of self-theologizing almost automatically meant a schism from the mother body and the formation of an "independent" church. Now, however, self-theologizing is taking place also within the traditional "mission" churches, Catholic and Protestant. The 1977 Apostolic Exhortation, *Catechesi Tradendae*, as well as various Protestant documents and publications, state quite frankly that the Christian faith has to be rethought, reformulated, and lived anew in each human culture. This approach breaks once and for all with the idea of the faith as "kernel" and of culture as the "husk." A more appropriate metaphor would be that of the flowering of a seed implanted into the soil of a particular culture.

Just as liberation theology does not imply a blanket endorsement of any cause anybody cares to declare holy, inculturation also has its limits. Inculturation has a *critical* dimension. The faith and its cultural expression are never completely coterminous. But then, this applies to the church in the West as much as it does to the church in the East and the South. In a very real sense, then, the Gospel is foreign to every culture and, likewise, inculturation is never a completed process. We should not, strictly speaking, use the past participle "inculturated." This is so not only because culture is not static, but also because the church may be led into previously unknown mysteries of the faith. Theology is always theology in the making, in the *process of* being contextualized and inculturated.

In our present situation yet another dimension has to be

added: just as we have always taken it for granted that the church in the Third World needs the church in the West, we are now discovering that the obverse is equally true. We all need each other; we influence, challenge, enrich, and invigorate each other. What we should be involved in, then, is not just "inculturation" but "interculturation."[5] A "homogeneous unit" church may become so in-grown that it believes its perspective on the Gospel to be the only legitimate one. The church must be a place to feel at home, but if only *we* feel at home in it, something has gone wrong. Local incarnations of the faith should not be *too* local. While acting locally, we have to think globally, in terms of the whole church.

Mission as Common Witness

The remark with which I concluded the previous paragraph hints at another characteristic of the emerging missionary paradigm: its intrinsic *ecumenical* nature. The evangelical awakenings at the end of the eighteenth century introduced the first ecumenical era into Protestantism. By the third decade of the nineteenth century, however, the fervor for cooperation had begun to peter out. It was only reintroduced at the beginning of the twentieth century; and from the very beginning, the new ecumenical era was intrinsically linked to mission. The first global manifestation of the ecumenical idea was the Edinburgh World Missionary Conference (1910). It was gradually beginning to dawn on Christians that authentic mission was impossible without authentic unity; likewise, it was inconceivable to divorce the church's obligation to take the Gospel to the whole world from its obligation to draw all Christ's people together.

The dichotomy, on the global structural level, between unity and mission was only overcome at the World Council of Churches New Delhi assembly (1961), where the International Missionary Council integrated with the WCC. The following year the Second Vatican Council met and its documents on the church, on mission, and on ecumenism underscored much of what has been developing in Protestantism. It is remarkable how Catholic documents have been modifying the manner in which they refer to Protestants: from calling them "heretics" or "schismatics," the appellations have been softened to "dissenters", "separated brethren" and, eventually, "brothers and sisters in Christ." The very word "mission," first applied to the Jesuit settlements in northern Germany, whose task it was to reconvert Lutherans to the Catholic church,[6] originally had an anti-Protestant ring to it. Even the praying of the Lord's Prayer together with Protestants was proscribed until 1949. In light of this, Vatican II represents a paradigm shift of major proportions in respect of Catholic-Protestant-Orthodox relations. James Crumley describes the adoption of the *Decree on Ecumenism* by the council as "the most important single event in the somewhat chequered history of the ecumenical movement."[7] It characterizes "the restoration of unity among all Christians" as a major concern of the council, since division among Christians "contradicts the will of Christ, scandalizes the world, and damages that most holy cause, the preaching of the Gospel to every creature." Likewise, ten years after the council, the apostolic exhortation *Evangelii Nuntiandi*, insisted on "a collaboration marked by a greater commitment to the Christian brethren with whom we are not yet united *in perfect unity.*"

The new reality finds expression, *inter alia*, in the term "*common witness.*"[8] The mutual coordination of mission and

unity is non-negotiable, not merely because of the new situation the church is facing in the world, but because God's people is one and its task in the world is one. It does not follow from this that all Christians will ever agree; however, disagreement should not be a reason for breaking off community. In the midst of all our diversity there is a center: Jesus Christ. And, ultimately, unity in mission and mission in unity do not merely serve the *church* but, through the church—the *sacramentum mundi*—stand in the service of *humankind* and seek to manifest *the cosmic rule of Christ.*[9] In the words of the 1989 CWME meeting in San Antonio: "The church is called again and again to be a prophetic sign and foretaste of the unity and renewal of the human family as envisioned in God's promised reign."

If we are honest, of course, we would have to admit that all of this is little more than eschatological lightning on a distant horizon. Both the "united church in mission" and the "unity of humankind" are, in a sense, fictions. But they constitute a vision that is indispensable if we want to do justice to what it means to be church, and to live creatively and missionally in the face of the eschatological tension that belongs to our very being as Christians.

Mission as Action in Hope

Ernst Troeltsch once said of nineteenth century (liberal) theology: "The eschatology office is mostly closed." One of the most striking characteristics of twentieth-century theology and missiology, however, is the rediscovery of eschatology, first in Protestantism, then in Catholicism. In our century the "eschatology office" has been working overtime.

The theology of the early church was, of course, eschatological through and through. Since the patristic period, however, the eschatological horizon became blurred. All "realist" models of eschatology were suppressed in mainline churches and relegated to sectarian fringes. In eighteenth and nineteenth-century Protestantism, for instance, the dominant eschatological view was postmillennial, a view which, in the Social Gospel movement, became almost entirely innerworldly. The twentieth century, however, saw a reopening of the eschatology office in virtually all branches of the Christian church—a circumstance that deeply influenced missionary thinking and practice as well. Ludwig Wiedenmann, for instance, argues that, since the 1930s, the entire field of German missiology may be characterized as "eschatological."[10] And what is true of German missiology has, in fact, become true of the entire ecumenical and Roman Catholic missionary movement as well. Gone is the optimism of the Social Gospel and of the "secular 1960s." There is a new awareness of crisis, of judgment, of the preliminary nature of our human endeavors, of the imminence of God's reign.

In twentieth-century evangelical circles, particularly in North America, an even more far-reaching eschatologization of mission has been taking place. The overriding purpose of mission here (it sometimes seems) is the preparation of people for the hereafter, ensuring for each a safe passage to heaven. The only real history is the history of missions: it is the hand on the clock of the world, telling us what time it is and when we may be expecting Christ's return. Once again—as was the case during the last two decades of the nineteenth century—the hearts of thousands of Christians are enkindled by the slogan about the evangelization of the world before the dawn of the new century, sometimes with the added notion of hastening Christ's return in this way.

And now, a few words about our Seminary...

1. Mission
Our clearest mission statement is the track record of our graduates: one study indicated that over 85 percent of them are in ministry--in the pastorate, on the mission field, and in other ministries. The priority of ministry is also expressed through Seminary initiatives like the Centre for Evangelism, the Centre for Intercultural Studies, and the guided self-evaluation of our Preparation for Ministry program.

2. Spirituality
It's ironic that the training of spiritual leaders often neglects their own spiritual nurture. One of the challenges we're facing head-on is that of taking responsibility for the spiritual growth of our students.

3. Community
Seminary is more than a place to take classes and meet a few like-minded people on the way to a degree. Our community, faculty and students, gives high priority to accessibility, relationships, worship, and accountability.

4. Programs
We offer Master of Divinity, Master of Religious Education, Master of Arts in Missiology, Master of Arts in Religion, and Doctor of Ministry degrees.

5. Connections
We're answerable. We are fully accredited by the Association of Theological Schools, and are affiliated with the University of Regina. We are also the official Seminary of the Christian and Missionary Alliance in Canada, assuring our students (from over 25 denominations) that our concern is for the real needs of the church.

Write or call the Director of Admissions for more information.

4400 Fourth Ave., Regina, Saskatchewan
Canada S4T 0H8
Phone (306) 545-1515

There can be no doubt that the contemporary rediscovery of the eschatological dimension of all authentic mission—even if it sometimes manifests itself in rather bizarre forms—is part of an emerging paradigm. There is today widespread agreement that eschatology determines the horizon of all Christian understanding, even if we are still groping for its precise meaning. We need an eschatology for mission that is *both* future-directed *and* oriented to the here and now, which holds in creative tension the "not yet" and the "already," justification as well as justice, the gospel of salvation and the gospel of liberation. Living in the force field of the assurance of salvation already received and the final victory already secured, the believer gets involved in the urgency of the task at hand.

The emerging eschatological perspective means that the world is no longer viewed as a hindrance: it is a challenge. This does not suggest any immanental, progressivistic, evolutionary concept of the reign of God as human product. Rather, it belongs to the essence of Christian teleology that it doubts that the eschatological vision can be fully realized in history.[11] God's transformation is different from human innovation. God takes us by

The mutual coordination of mission and unity is non-negotiable because God's people is one and its task in the world is one.

surprise. God is always before us, the coming triumph bidding us to follow—as Beker has so lucidly illustrated in respect of Paul's theology.[12] From this perspective, then, the future holds the primacy. The ultimate triumph remains uniquely God's gift. It is *God* who makes all things new (Rev. 21:5). If we turn off the lighthouse of eschatology we can only grope around in darkness and despair. And it is precisely the vision of God's triumph that makes it impossible to look for sanctuary in quietism, neutrality, or withdrawal from the world.

We do distinguish between hope for the ultimate and perfect on the one hand, and hope for the penultimate and approximate, on the other. We make this distinction under protest, with pain, and at the same time with realism. We perform our mission in hope. So, if Margull was correct in referring to the evangelistic dimension of our missionary calling as *hope in action*, it may be appropriate to label mission in the context of our eschatological expectation as *action in hope*.[13] Witnessing to the gospel of present salvation and future hope we are identifying with the awesome birth pangs of God's new creation.

Notes

1. Hendrik Kraemer, *Uit de nalatenschap van dr H. Kraemer* (Kok: Kampen, 1970), p. 70. This contribution was first published in 1959.
2. Cf. Thomas S. Kuhn, *The Structure of Scientific Revolutions* (Chicago: Univ. of Chicago Press, 1970; 2nd edition, enlarged); Hans Küng, *Theologie im Aufbruch* (Munich: Piper Verlag, 1987).
3. J. L. Segundo, *The Liberation of Theology* (Maryknoll: Orbis Books, 1976), pp. 7–38.
4. Cf. Per Frostin, *Liberation Theology in Tanzania and South Africa: A First World Perspective* (Lund: Lund Univ. Press, 1988), p. 6f.
5. Thus Joseph Blomjous, (reference in Aylward Shorter, *Toward a Theology of Inculturation* [Maryknoll: Orbis Books, 1988], pp. 13-16).
6. Cf. Josef Glazik, "Die neuzeitliche Mission under der Leitung der Propaganda-Kongregation," in *Warum Mission?*, Vol. 1 (St. Ottilien: EOS-Verlag, 1984), p. 29.
7. James Crumley, "Reflections on Twenty-Five Years After the Decree on Ecumenism," *Ecumenical Trends* 18 (1989); 146.
8. Cf. *Common Witness: A Study Document of the Joint Working Group of the Roman Catholic Church and the World Council of Churches* (Geneva: World Council of Churches, 2nd Printing, 1984).
9. Cf. W. A. Saayman, *Unity and Mission* (Pretoria: Univ. of South Africa, 1984), pp. 21–55.
10. Ludwig Wiedenmann, *Mission und Eschatologie: Eine Analyse der neueren deutschen Missionstheologie* (Paderborn: Verlag Bonifacius-Druckerei, 1965).
11. Cf. Max Stackhouse, *Apologia: Contextualization, Globalization, and Mission in Theological Education* (Grand Rapids: Wm. B. Eerdmans Publishing Co., 1988), p. 206.
12. Cf. J. C. Beker, *Paul the Apostle: The Triumph of God in Life and Thought* (Philadelphia: Fortress Press 1980); and *Paul's Apocalyptic Gospel* (Philadelphia: Fortress Press, 1984).
13. Hans Margull, *Hope in Action: The Church's Task in the World* (Philadelphia: Muhlenberg, 1962).

The Pentecostal/Charismatic Contribution to World Evangelization

L. Grant McClung, Jr.

What would surprise Frank and Andrew Crouch most about "Mission in the 1990s" is the fact that their spiritual family—the modern pentecostal/charismatic movement—has made it this far. When the Crouch families left the United States for Egypt in 1912, they expected their stay to be a short one since, in their anticipation, the Lord would return at any moment.[1] The radical obedience characterizing thousands of "missionaries of the one-way ticket" in the formative years of pentecostalism accounts for the explosive growth of the most rapidly expanding expression of the Christian church as we approach the end of the century of its birth.

From the beginning we pentecostals have been a strange breed, locked in a time warp between the past and the future. When supernatural phenomena burst on the scene at the turn of the twentieth century, pentecostals were certain that they were living in the end time restoration of New Testament apostolic power. They reasoned that signs and wonders were a portent of Christ's imminent return. Little wonder, then, that they took off with such explosive dynamism.[2]

Now, joined by our charismatic cousins in the closing quarter of this century, the combined movements, says researcher David B. Barrett, come in an amazing variety of 38 categories, 11,000 pentecostal denominations and 3,000 independent charismatic denominations spread across 8,000 ethnolinguistic cultures and 7,000 languages![3] Given this variety, a monolithic, homogeneous pentecostal/charismatic perspective on mission in this last decade of the century is not realistic, though there are common threads that make up the fabric of the pentecostal/charismatic experience.[4]

Some of the more prominent features of this tradition are noteworthy (mid-1988 appraisal):

- 332 million affiliated church members worldwide (updated by Barrett to 351 million by July 1989);
- 19 million new members a year;
- 54,000 new members a day;
- $34 billion annually donated to Christian causes;
- active in 80 percent of the world's 3,300 large metropolises;
- 66 percent of membership is in the Third World.[5]

Barrett's cross section of worldwide pentecostalism reveals a composite "international pentecostal/charismatic" who is more urban than rural, more female than male, more Third World (66 percent) than Western world, more impoverished (87 percent) than affluent, more family oriented than individualistic, and, on average younger than eighteen.[6]

Yet, with the rapid growth and diversity, there seem to be at least four main characteristics of pentecostals and charismatics in the way we will do mission in the 1990s. The 1990s will be a decade of *definition, discipleship, deterrence/distraction,* and *"Divine surprise."*

A Decade of Definition

Biblical authority determines the beginning point for pentecostal/charismatic missions theology and strategizing, even if this comes in the form of informal oral theology of illiterate pentecostals in many parts of the southern world.[7] Though middle-class theologians and ideologues in academic circles may relax previously held theological positions, practitioners who are getting the job done will continue to emulate biblical commands and models in their missions practice. The book of Acts, for example, has long been the basic textbook for ministry practice and is believed by the rank and file in pentecostal/charismatic congregations to have a didactic, intentional purpose for today's Christian.[8]

One of the misrepresentations of our tradition is that we are a "Spirit movement" at the expense of a firm, biblical Christology in the tradition of historical theology. Nothing could be further from the truth. It is our confession that the presence of the Holy Spirit will only give more and more honor to the unique and indispensable revelation of God in the powerfully present person of the Lord Jesus Christ. Arthur F. Glasser relates this witness of the Holy Spirit to the Lordship of Christ in pentecostal/charismatic spirituality:

> Many evangelicals have been challenged by the immediacy and reality of God that Pentecostals reflect along with their freedom and unabashed willingness to confess openly their allegiance to Christ. The achievements of their churches are equally impressive, reflecting their settled conviction that the full experience of the Holy Spirit will not only move the Church closer to Jesus at its center, but at the same time, press the Church to move out into the world in mission.[9]

Pentecostal and charismatic theology maintains the necessity of the baptism in the Holy Spirit as the indispensable enduement of power for Christian mission (Luke 24:49; Acts 1:8), that Jesus, the exalted mediator between God and man, is the Baptizer in the Holy Spirit (Matt. 3:11; Mark 1:8; Luke 3:16; John 1:33), and that Jesus Christ continues today to do all that he began in his earthly mission (Acts 1:1).[10] They would confess the trinitarian proclamation of Peter, "Being therefore exalted at the right

L. Grant McClung, Jr., a former missionary to Europe, is Assistant Professor of Missions and Church Growth at the Church of God School of Theology in Cleveland, Tennessee, and Adjunct Professor of Church Growth at Fuller Theological Seminary School of World Mission.

hand of God, and having received from the Father the promise of the Holy Spirit, [Jesus] has poured out this which you see and hear" (Acts 2:33).

In one of the more recent studies on the dynamics of evangelical growth in Latin America, British social scientist David Martin speaks of the proliferation of pentecostals there. "In Guatemala City," he notes, "you can hardly fail to notice the number of public buses decorated with evangelical texts."[11] Martin observes the frequency of the visible assertion, "*Jesus Salva*" (Jesus Saves) across storefront churches in villages and urban barrios in every Latin American country. What the pentecostals are telling us is that Jesus, and *Jesus alone*, saves. As a populist movement centered on the person of Christ, pentecostals in the Two-Thirds World should not be expected to jump on the bandwagon of interreligious dialogue. They will continue to clearly define their distinctives through the 1990s.

Pentecostals and charismatics will also continue to tell their own story and move toward a definition of a distinctive pentecostal/charismatic missiology. Melvin L. Hodges of the Assemblies of God was the lone pentecostal who sought to articulate a pentecostal missiology, especially in the era of pentecostal expansion following World War II. His name became synonymous with indigenous church principles, and he was a regular dialogue partner with nonpentecostal missiologists.[12]

With encouragement from nonpentecostal observers Hodges continued to publish occasionally, but the missiological literary reflection by pentecostals was minimal through the 1960s and 1970s. David Hesselgrave analyzed the scarcity of articles on missiology written in two journals from 1965 to 1986 specifically from a pentecostal/charismatic orientation. Of 949 articles presented in the *International Review of Mission* during those twenty-one years, only 17 (or 1.8%) were from this tradition. Of 604 articles during the same years in *Evangelical Missions Quarterly*, a meager 2 (or .3%) from pentecostals were printed.[13]

This trend changed in the 1980s. The seeds of pentecostal missiology unwittingly planted by Roland Allen and A. B. Simpson (see McGee, *Dictionary*, pp. 620–21) and nurtured by Melvin Hodges began to sprout in a proliferation of articles and books by insiders who claimed that the primary purpose and self-identity of the pentecostal movement centered on a revival raised up by God for world evangelization.[14]

Along the way, the seedlings profited from the greenhouse of the Church Growth Movement, although Donald McGavran and his colleagues were not the first to call attention to the outstanding growth of pentecostal missions. In 1943 J. Merle Davis (in an International Missionary Council study) pointed to pentecostal growth in Latin America in his *How The Church Grows in Brazil*, and in 1954 Lesslie Newbigin suggested in *The Household of God* (Friendship Press) that pentecostals be seen as "The Community of The Holy Spirit" (Chap. 4).[15]

In this "Decade of Definition" there will be a rapid growth in the science of pentecostal/charismatic studies and enough missiological literature to support what I feel is the emergence of a definitive pentecostal/charismatic missiology.[16] As Donald W. Dayton has so aptly stated, the pentecostal/charismatic movement has a unique identity. "I am suggesting," he observed in his address to the American Society of Missology, "that Pentecostalism ought to be studied as *Pentecostalism*, without the assumptions created by assuming it to be a part of a larger genus called 'evangelicalism.'"[17] "I prefer the language of the 'third force,'" he said, "and see the movement as a corrective to the classical traditions of Christian faith."[18]

Hopefully there will be continued corrections and expansions to the theological stories and self-examination of classical pentecostalism done primarily through the post-World War II cadre of mainline North American pentecostal scholars who may have been pushed into a polemical corner on one hand or lauded with acceptance from evangelicals on the other. The theological story of mainline North American pentecostalism still has too much of an evangelical accent and needs to be rediscovered in a fresh pentecostal/charismatic hermeneutic. After all, claims Paul Pomerville, "An inordinate 'silence on the Holy Spirit' is part of the Protestant mission heritage. The Pentecostal Movement addresses that silence in a significant way."[19]

There will be a continued breaking of the silence as charismatics and non-North Atlantic pentecostals postulate their understanding of the mission of the church in the 1990s. Where are the "Melvin Hodges" of the pentecostal/charismatic world in Asia, Africa, and Latin America (and in the newly visible churches of Eastern Europe and the Soviet Union—where for years there

> 5000 charismatic leaders will gather in July 1991 for the International Charismatic Congress on World Evangelism—a Charismatic Lausanne II?

have been more Christians, many of them pentecostal, than members of the Communist party)? When their voices are heard in leading missiological journals, the whole landscape of the missions agenda will change. Traditional pentecostals and nonpentecostals alike may be in for a surprise![20]

The Decade of Self-Definition by pentecostals and charismatics may help to correct the negative assumptions of outside observers—assumptions such as excessive emotionalism, prioritizing personal experience over Scripture, a preoccupation with tongues, demons, and the miraculous, a minimal if nonexistent social concern.[21] This is not to suggest that pentecostals and charismatics are to be so exclusive as to be above correction from the body of Christ. (We are, too often, prone toward arrogance and triumphalism due to an inflated sense of destiny!)

What will come to light, however, as we hear more case studies from pentecostal/charismatic churches, is that the "broader mission" of the church has been part and parcel of this branch of the family as an automatic outgrowth of our prioritization of "Great Commission" missions, conversion, evangelization, and church planting. Pentecostal pastor Juan Sepulveda of Chile states:

> Pentecostalism—in spite of its popular origin—did not develop a social ethic which would encourage the participation of believers in social, labor union or political organizations, which promote social change. This does not mean that Pentecostalism failed to have any social impact. Rather to the contrary, the Pentecostal communities meant a powerful offering of life-meaning for wide sectors excluded from our societies.[22]

"What is overlooked," says William Menzies, "is that Pentecostals have quietly gone about social renewal in unobtrusive ways, working with the poor of this world in unheralded corners."[23]

When social activist Ronald Sider gathered representatives from the evangelical and pentecostal/charismatic communities for a dialogue on social action, there was an interesting blend of "Words, Works, and Wonders" seen in the pentecostal/charismatic churches.[24] The nonpentecostal world cannot afford to typecast all pentecostals and charismatics (especially internationally) into the affluent Hollywood media images we saw during the heyday of TV charisma in the 1980s.[25] Pentecostals and charismatics are more politically and socially involved than most casual observers suppose, but their main priority on evangelization will continue through this decade.[26]

A Decade of Discipleship

The language of countdown and closure toward the year 2000 is being spoken by classical mainline pentecostals and charismatics alike. Older groups have general denominational emphases for the decade: "Into The Harvest" (Church of God, Cleveland); "Target 2000" (Pentecostal Holiness Church); "Decade of Harvest" (Assemblies of God). Their goals are ambitious.[27]

The charismatics are also enthusiastic in stating their goals to see the majority of the human race Christian by the end of the century. The North American Congress on the Holy Spirit and World Evangelization filled the Hoosier Dome in Indianapolis, Indiana, from August 15–19, 1990, under the impatient theme, "Evangelize the World, Now!" Under the umbrella of the North American Renewal Service Committee (NARSC), charismatics of every stripe are targeting world evangelization as priority number one.[28] Working with international networks of charismatics, they will gather 5,000 charismatic leaders together in Brighton, England for the International Charismatic Congress on World Evangelization in July 1991 (a charismatic Lausanne II?). The mushrooming growth of independent charismatic churches is one of the most promising developments in the 1980s that will impact the world of missiology in the 1990s. In North America, they represent the fastest growing segment of American Christianity: scholarly estimates place their number at 60,000 to 100,000 congregations (and they are still multiplying). "Charismatic ministers and lay people are getting more and more interested in missions. More and more charismatic churches are hiring mission directors and sending out missionaries nowadays," says Fuller School of World Mission researcher Edward K. Pousson. In a landmark study that will greatly serve the church upon its publication, Pousson charted the "Origins, Aspects and Missionary Activities of Independent Charismatic Churches and Ministries Based in the U.S.A." (unpublished doctoral diss., March 1990).[29]

Seeking to build an exchange and service network among these groups, Howard Foltz founded the Association of International Missions Services (AIMS) in the late 1980s. At their annual conference in October, 1989, AIMS launched their "Decade of Destiny" emphasis calling on 5,000 charismatic churches to become involved in missions work in the 1990s. They also, "agreed to target every unreached people group in the world for adoption by at least one local church and to emphasize the need for churches to set a specific budget earmarked for helping unreached peoples groups."[30]

A Decade of Deterrence and Distraction

At this juncture I must raise cautions and concerns I have for the mission of the church in the 1990s, especially as it is understood by the pentecostal/charismatic community of faith. I choose the words "deterrence" and "distraction" to reflect the external and internal challenges to the vitality of our mission.

To *deter* is "to prevent or discourage (someone) from acting or proceeding by arousing fear, uncertainty." Interestingly, the word is from the same root (*terrere*) as the word *terror*.[31] For all of the positive prognostications for the 1990s, an explosive, latent countercurrent is growing.[32] Consider the mixture of the burgeoning growth of the pentecostal/charismatic expression as the "second most widespread variety of Christian spiritual lifestyle"[33] contrasted with the membership losses of previously dominant religious movements. Consider the aggressive pentecostal/charismatic "to the gates of hell"[34] evangelistic mentality contrasted by an equally determined missionary fervor and growing intolerance from cults and non-Christian religions. These contrasts make for one result: religious persecution.

A survey of literature on mission in the 1990s produces interesting terms and concepts: "Christian uniqueness," "global economic realities," "ecological crisis," "inculturation," "inter-

---

Will North American "Baby Boomer" charismatics fall prey to a preoccupation with material prosperity?

---

religious dialogue," "liberation," "unreached people," "rapprochement." One word is obviously absent: *martyrdom.* Not that anyone should wish that experience on anyone ("The spiritual gift," someone quipped, "that is used only once!"). The fact is that the 1990s will be a decade of deterrence in which David Barrett's estimate of 260,000 annual Christian martyrs may unfortunately multiply.[35]

Pentecostals and charismatics believe that the primary source of deterrence is spiritual. They would echo the sentiments of Neuza Itioka that, "Certainly one of the most important issues worldwide missions must face in the 1990s is how to confront the destructive supernatural evil forces that oppose the missionary enterprise."[36] For this reason, expect the proliferation of "power literature" and publications on spiritual warfare to continue. It is currently one of the most frequent topics in pentecostal/charismatic publications.[37]

Still, the greatest challenge may come from within in what may be a decade of distraction. There are always the twin perils of triumphalism and elitism, says Russell Spittler, who relates the insights of University of Chicago church historian Martin Marty. Marty, says Spittler, "once observed that Pentecostals used to argue God's approval upon them because they numbered so few. But more recently, he said, the proof has shifted to the fact that there are so many."[38]

Can pentecostals and charismatics survive their own success? Will North American "Baby Boomer" charismatics fall prey to a preoccupation with material prosperity and an "overrealized eschatology" in wanting the "Kingdom Now"?[39] Yuppie sub-urban pentecostals in North America (well-"heeled" but need-ing "healing" from monocultural myopia) may have bought Michelob's pronouncement for the 1980s, "You can have it all!"[40]

Can pentecostal/charismatic superleaders remember their humble roots and avoid becoming drunk with materialism, con-sumerism, and ecclesiastical power? Will the vertically oriented pentecostal/charismatic leadership structures make room for needed lay leadership from the female, urban, non-Western, younger, and the impoverished "international pentecostal composite" described by Barrett? Can the "urgent missiology" fired by an eschatological expectation of the Day of the Lord be transmitted to this new generation of pentecostals and charismatics?[41] Will there be any "missionaries of the one-way ticket" in the 1990s? Will there be, in sociologist Max Weber's terms, a "routini-zation of charisma"?[42]

A Decade of Divine Surprise

In the end, the Christian church, pentecostals and charismatics included, will discover that the 1990s will be *God's decade*. The glory of the Christian mission and harvest (Matthew 9:38) will be God's alone. In spite of all our strategy conferences, consultations, and theological reflections as we labor together *with* God as agents of reconciliation (1 Cor. 3:9; 2 Cor. 5:18), all branches of the Chris-tian tradition will be awed by the initiative (Acts 13:1–4) and the unpredictability of God in mission (Acts 8:26ff.; 9:10ff.; 10:9ff.). *Charismata* cannot be contained.

As he did for the curious disciples wanting to forecast their future (Acts 1:6), the Lord of mission reminds us that it is not ours "to know the times or dates" but to "receive power when the Holy Spirit comes on you" (Acts 1:7–8 NIV). With our talk of "dialogue" and "trialogue" we are overdue for "Pneumalogue"—hearing what the Spirit is saying to the churches.

Notes

1. Eugene N. Hastie, *History of the West Central District Council of the Assemblies of God* (Fort Dodge, Iowa: Walterick Printing Co., 1948), p. 143.
2. L. Grant McClung, Jr., "New Cultures. New Challenges. New Church?" *Pentecostals From the Inside Out*, Harold B. Smith, ed. (Whea-ton, Ill.; Victor Books/Christianity Today, 1990), p. 105.
3. David B. Barrett, "Statistics, Global," *Dictionary of Pentecostal and Charismatic Movements*, Stanley M. Burgess and Gary B. McGee, eds. (Grand Rapids, Mich.: Zondervan Publishing House, 1988), p. 811.
4. See Gary B. McGee, "Assemblies of God Mission Theology: A Historical Perspective," *International Bulletin of Missionary Research* 10, no. 4 (1986): 166–70, and L. Grant McClung, Jr., "Theology and Strategy of Pentecostal Missions," *International Bulletin of Missionary Research* 12, no. 1 (1988): 2–6.
5. David B. Barrett, "The Twentieth-Century Pentecostal/Charismatic Renewal in The Holy Spirit, With Its Goal of World Evangelization," *International Bulletin of Missionary Research* 12, no. 3 (1988): 119–29.
6. Ibid. Also repeated in the Burgess and McGee *Dictionary* article (note 3).
7. Eugene Nida describes Latin American pentecostals as the "Church of the Dirty Bibles." The Bible is used frequently in worship services, being read along by the poor with their fingers.
8. See L. Grant McClung, Jr., *Azusa Street and Beyond: Pentecostal Missions and Church Growth in The Twentieth Century* (South Plainfield, N.J.: Bridge Publishing, 1986), pp. 48–54; Paul A. Pomerville, *The Third

Force in Missions* (Peabody, Mass.: Hendrickson Publishers, 1985); F. J. May, *The Book of Acts and Church Growth* (Cleveland, Tenn.: Pathway Press, 1990); French L. Arrington, *The Acts of the Apostles: Introduction, Translation and Commentary* (Peabody Mass.: Hendrickson Publishers 1989); Delmer R. and Eleanor R. Guynes, *The Apostolic Nature of The Church* (Kuala Lumpur, Malaysia: Calvary Church Press, 1986); B. E. Underwood, *Sixteen New Testament Principles For World Evangelization* (Franklin Springs, Ga.: Advocate Press, 1988); Harold R. Carpenter, *Mandate and Mission* (Springfield, Mo.: Central Bible College Press, 1988).
9. Arthur F. Glasser in Foreword to Pomerville, *The Third Force in Mis-sions*, p. vii.
10. One of the better studies exploring the "fourfold gospel" of Jesus as Savior, Baptizer, Healer, and Soon Coming King found in pente-costal theology is discussed in Donald W. Dayton, *Theological Roots of Pentecostalism* (Grand Rapids, Mich.: Zondervan Publishing House, 1987).
11. David Martin, "Speaking in Latin Tongues," *National Review*, Sep-tember 29, 1989; see also "The Hidden Fire," an interview with Martin by Tim Stafford, *Christianity Today*, May 14, 1990, and Martin's complete study (352 pp.), *Tongues of Fire: The Explosion of Protestantism in Latin America* (Cambridge, Mass.: Basil Blackwell, Inc., 1990).
12. Cf. Melvin L. Hodges, *A Theology of the Church and Its Mission: A Pentecostal Perspective* (Springfield, Mo.: Gospel Publishing House, 1977), and *The Indigenous Church and the Missionary* (South Pasadena: William Carey Library, 1978); see also a partial list of Hodges' writings in McClung, *Azusa Street and Beyond*, pp. 200–201, and articles by Gary B. McGee ("Hodges, Melvin Lyle," pp. 403–44, "Missions, Overseas," pp. 610–25) in the Burgess/McGee *Dictionary*.
13. *Today's Choices for Tomorrow's Mission* (Grand Rapids, Mich.: Zonder-van Publishing House, 1988). Hesselgrave includes an entire chapter on pentecostals/charismatics, calling them, "perhaps the most mis-sionary-minded segment of world Christianity" (p. 118).
14. In addition to other publications listed in Notes 1–12, the following are examples of the growing list since 1986: C. Peter Wagner, *Spiritual Power and Church Growth* (Altamonte Springs, Fla.: Creation House, 1986)—a rewrite of Wagner's original *Look Out! The Pentecostals Are Coming*, Creation House 1973); John Wimber, *Power Evangelism* (San Francisco, Calif.: Harper and Row, 1986); Gary B. McGee, *This Gospel Shall Be Preached: A History and Theology of Assemblies of God Foreign Missions to 1959*, vol. 1 (Springfield, Mo.: Gospel Publishing House, 1986); vol. 2 appeared in 1989; *International Review of Mission* 75, nos. 297–98 (1986)—special issues on pentecostals and charismatics in mis-sion, coordinated by Walter J. Hollenweger; Vinson Synan, *The Twen-tieth-Century Pentecostal Explosion* (Altamonte Springs, Fla.: Creation House, 1987); James R. Goff, Jr., *Fields White Unto Harvest: Charles F. Parham and the Missionary Origins of Pentecostalism* (Fayetteville, Ark.: The Univ. of Arkansas Press, 1988); articles by Russell Spittler, "Implicit Values in Pentecostal Missions," and Gary B. McGee, "Assemblies of God Overseas Missions: Foundations For Recent Growth," in *Missiology: An International Review* 16, no. 4 (1988); James T. Guyton, *Dynamics of Pentecostal Church Growth* (Cleveland, Tenn.: Pathway Press, 1989); Margaret M. Poloma, *The Assemblies of God at the Crossroads: Charisma and Institutional Dilemmas* (Knoxville, Tenn.: Univ. of Tennessee Press, 1989); David Shibley, *A Force in The Earth: The Charismatic Renewal and World Evangelism* (Altamonte Springs, Fla.: Creation House, 1989); Byron Klaus, Murray, Dempster, and Doug Peterson, *Called and Empowered: Pentecostal Perspectives on Global Mis-sion* (Peabody, Mass.: Hendrickson Publishers, 1990).
15. More on this symbiotic relationship is found in part four of my *Azusa Street and Beyond* (pp. 109–118) and "From *Bridges* to *Waves*: Pen-tecostals and the Church Growth Movement," *Pneuma: The Journal of the Society for Pentecostal Studies*, Spring 1985, pp. 5–18.
16. Walter J. Hollenweger notes, for example, that the University of Utrecht in Holland will establish a chair in Pentecostal studies in 1991 (per-sonal correspondence with the author, March 3, 1990). No doubt other schools will follow this trend and the example set by Hollenweger's

mentoring of studies on pentecostalism during his tenure at the University of Birmingham, England. See "Dissertation Notices" in the *International Bulletin of Missionary Research* 14, no. 2 (1990): 94, for some of this work.

17. Donald W. Dayton, "The Holy Spirit and Christian Expansion in The Twentieth Century," *Missiology: An International Review* 16, no. 4 (1988): 402.

18. Ibid., p. 403.

19. Paul Pomerville, *The Third Force in Missions,* p. 3.

20. In this light many of the views from non-North American pentecostals and charismatics in the *International Review of Mission* series are informative (see note 14). See also Juan Sepulveda (Chile), "Reflections on the Pentecostal Contribution to the Mission of the Church in Latin America" (unpub. Spanish paper translated by Dr. James Beaty, Dean, Church of God School of Theology, Cleveland, Tenn.).

21. Cf. Arthur Glasser, *International Bulletin of Missionary Research* 13, no. 1 (1989): 5, and Eugene L. Stockwell, *International Review of Mission* 75, no. 298 (1986): 114–15.

22. Sepulveda, "Reflections on the Pentecostal Contribution," p. 9.

23. William Menzies, "Current Pentecostal Theology of the End Times," *The Pentecostal Minister* 8, no. 3 (1988): 9.

24. Ronald Sider, ed., "Words, Works and Wonders: Papers from an International Dialogue between the Pentecostal/Charismatic Renewal and Evangelical Social Action," *Transformation* 5, no. 4 (1988).

25. See Quentin J. Schultze, "The Great Transmission," *Pentecostals From the Inside Out*, pp. 93–104, and articles on "Evangelism," "Bakker, James Orren (Jim) and Tammy Faye (La Valley)," and "Swaggart, Jimmy Lee" in the Burgess/McGee *Dictionary*.

26. See the following for just a sampling of reports and case studies on pentecostal/charismatic social involvement: Margaret M. Poloma, "Pentecostals and Politics in North and Central America," *Prophetic Religions and Politics: Religion and The Political Order*, vol. 1, Jeffrey K. Hadden and Anson Shupe, eds. (New York: Paragon House, 1986), pp. 329–52; Paul Brink, "Las Acacias Evangelical Pentecostal Church, Caracas, Venezuela," *Urban Mission* 7, no. 3 (1990): 46–50; Brian Bird, "Reclaiming the Urban War Zones," *Christianity Today*, January 15, 1990, pp. 16–20; Ron Williams, ed., *Foursquare World Advance* 26, no. 3 (1990)—issue on social concerns; Irving Hexham and Karla Poewe-Hexham, "Charismatics and Apartheid," in *Charisma and Christian Life*, May 1990, pp. 62–70; Thomas Fritch, "It Started at the Dumpster," *Urban Mission* 7, no. 5 (1990): 54–57 (dealing with an Assembly of God local church ministry to the homeless).

27. The Assemblies of God, for example, hope to enlist one million prayer partners, plant 5,000 new churches, train 20,000 new ministers, and receive five million new converts in the United States alone this decade. See "Our Mission for the 90s," *Pentecostal Evangel*, January 1, 1989.

28. See *A.D. 2000 Together*, available from 237 North Michigan Street, South Bend, Indiana 46601.

29. David Shibley calls the charismatics "Missions Awakening Giant" (chap. two of his *A Force in The Earth*) yet claims, "world evangelization can never be accomplished by charismatics alone. Neither can it be realized without us" (p. 26). Shibley, world missions director for Church on the Rock in Rockwall, Texas (pastored by Larry Lea) is one of the first among the charismatic movement to intentionally apply the vigor of the charismatic renewal to world evangelization. The 1990s will see a growth of literature like his, as well as academic studies such as Pousson's.

30. "Charismatic Missions Charge Into the '90s," *Charisma and Christian Life*, January 1990, p. 27.

31. "Deter," in *the Reader's Digest Great Encyclopedic Dictionary* (Pleasantville, N.Y.: The Reader's Digest Association, 1966), p. 363.

32. The first year of this decade has been encouraging: the end of totalitarianism in Europe, advances in human rights in South Africa, encouraging political developments in Central America. Christians in the capitalistic West, however, may have a false sense of euphoria in that, for example, the Cold War is over and the threat of communism

weakened. One must be reminded that "Democratization is not Evangelization," that there remain crying needs in the Soviet Union and Eastern Europe, that Third World debt, ecological disasters, the squalor of deplorable urban environments and the despair of the poor continue to be powder kegs for new social challenges in this decade.

33. Russell P. Spittler, "Maintaining Distinctives: The Future of Pentecostalism," *Pentecostals from the Inside Out*, p. 121.

34. Seen, for example, in Ron Steele, *Plundering Hell To Populate Heaven—the Reinhard Bonnke Story* (Melbourne, Fla.: Dove Christian Books, 1988). Bonnke, the German evangelist known for his 34,000-seat tent and massive crowds, has vowed to spread the Gospel "From Cape Town to Cairo."

35. David Barrett, "Getting Ready for Mission in the 1990s," *Missiology: An International Review* 15, no. 1 (1987): 13; "Forecasting the Future in World Mission: Some Future Faces of Missions," *Missiology: An International Review* 15, no. 4 (1987): 442; "Annual Statistical Table on Global Mission: 1990," *International Bulletin of Missionary Research* 14, no. 1 (1990): 27.

36. *International Bulletin of Missionary Research* 14, no. 1 (1990): 8.

37. Kevin Springer, ed., *Power Encounters Among Christians in the Western World* (San Francisco, Calif.: Harper and Row, 1988); John White, *When the Spirit Comes in Power: Signs and Wonders Among God's People* (Downer's Grove: Ill.: InterVarsity Press, 1988); Don Williams, *Signs, Wonders, and the Kingdom of God: A Biblical Guide for the Reluctant Skeptic* (Ann Arbor, Mich.: Servant Publications, 1989); Charles H. Kraft, *Christianity With Power: Your Worldview and Your Experience of the Supernatural* (Ann Arbor, Mich.: Servant Publications, 1989); John Dawson, *Taking Our Cities for God* (Altamonte Springs, Fla.: Creation House, 1989); Opal L. Reddin, ed., *Power Encounter: A Pentecostal Perspective* (Springfield, Mo.: Central Bible College Press, 1989); Steven Lawson, "Defeating Territorial Spirits," and John Dawson, "Winning the Battle for Your Neighborhood," in *Charisma and Christian Life*, April 1990, pp. 47–61; C. Peter Wagner and F. Douglas Pennoyer, eds., *Wrestling With Dark Angels* (Ventura, Calif.: Regal Books, 1990). The spectacular title may obscure the contents of this compilation of papers and responses presented during the Academic Symposium on Power Evangelism at Fuller Seminary School of World Mission on December 13–15, 1988. Forty scholars representing some twenty institutions of higher learning attended.

38. Spittler, "Maintaining Distinctives," p. 122.

39. In chapter 8 of *A Force in the Earth* ("The Why of the Prosperity Message"), Shibley gives a balanced critique of the health and wealth gospel and makes the bold claim that the prosperity message has been given to the church in the 1980s in order to fund the massive strides needed in the 1990s. See also James R. Goff, Jr., "Questions of Health and Wealth," *Pentecostals From the Inside Out*, pp. 65–80.

40. Art Levine, "Lifestyle: Having It All," *U.S. News and World Report*, January 1, 1990, 112–113.

41. See William D. Faupel, "This Gospel of the Kingdom: The Significance of Eschatology in the Development of Pentecostal Thought" (unpub. doctoral diss. from the University of Birmingham, England, 1989); L. Grant McClung, Jr., "The Forgotten Sign of The Times," *The Pentecostal Minister* 8, no. 3 (1988): 11–14, and "Salvation Shock Troops," in *Pentecostals From the Inside Out*, pp. 81–90.

42. Margaret M. Poloma, *The Assemblies of God at the Crossroads*, p. 6.

DOCTOR OF MINISTRY
FOR MISSIONARIES
DENVER SEMINARY

Provides Flexibility in Scheduling

- **Extension Correspondence Courses**   8 quarter units
  (to be done on the field)

- **Summer Seminars**   15 quarter units
  (offered consecutively in odd-numbered years)

- **Residence Study**   16 quarter units
  8 quarter units may be completed at any
    accredited seminary
  8 quarter units must be completed at Denver Seminary

- **Professional Project**   10 quarter units
  (to be done on the field)

- **Oral Exam and Integrative Essay**

M.Div. or equivalent required

We also offer a separate track for pastors.

All inquiries for further information on the Doctor of Ministry program should be addressed to:

Director, Doctor of Ministry Program
Denver Seminary
P.O. Box 10,000
Denver, CO 80210
303-761-2482
1-800-922-3040
Fax: 303-761-8060

Denver Seminary admits students of any race, sex, color,
and national or ethnic origin.

DENVER SEMINARY

The Status of the Christian World Mission in the 1990s

David B. Barrett

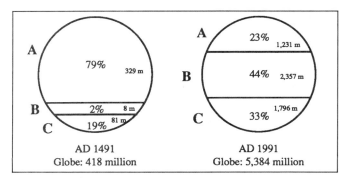

AD 1491
Globe: 418 million

AD 1991
Globe: 5,384 million

Mission is Contact

The table opposite is designed to help us monitor the progress of world mission. Mission is all about Christians being in contact with non-Christians. If there is no such contact, there is no mission going on. (When Christians minister to other Christians, it is better to term it ministry or pastoralia, reserving "mission" for contact with non-Christians.) The status of the world Christian mission today as compared to five centuries ago is depicted in the accompanying diagram, which divides our globe into three worlds based on how much mission contact exists. World C consists of all those who individually call themselves Christian (line 9 opposite). Worlds B and A cover all who individually are identified as other than Christian (line 19 opposite). World B stands for non-Christians who are in contact with Christians and who have at least some knowledge of Christ and the Gospel. World A stands for non-Christians who have never come in contact with Christians and have no knowledge of Christ and the Gospel (line 71 opposite).

Up until five hundred years ago there was almost no contact between the three major races: Caucasoid, Mongoloid, and Negroid. Some 93% of all Christians then were Whites in Europe. This means that at that time World C was virtually a racial ghetto out of touch with the non-Christian world (almost all of which was in World A, with a mere 2% in World B).

Contact in the 1990s

Five hundred years later, that picture has radically changed. Mass communication, mass transportation, mass migration, and the resultant religious pluralism have put all the races in daily contact almost everywhere on earth. Christians (World C) are now found in some 10,000 different ethnolinguistic peoples; in half of these they form the majority. Christians today are sufficiently in contact with World B—through presence, witness, evangelism, local church outreach, social action, foreign missions, liberation, interreligious dialogue, etc.—for us to describe its 2.3 billion inhabitants as aware of Christ and the Gospel.

However, World A, consisting of 1.2 billion people (see lines 71–73 opposite), remains untouched by Christian missionaries, mission agencies, or the world's 2.6 million local churches.

David B. Barrett, a contributing editor, has been an ordained missionary of the Church Missionary Society since 1956. Anglican Research Officer since 1970, he is currently Research Consultant to the Southern Baptist Foreign Mission Board; research director, Charismatic Renewal in the Mainline Churches; and Vatican Consultant on world evangelization.

The long-term trend is alarming. The globe's population out of touch with Christians has risen from 329 million in A.D. 1491 to 1.2 billion today. And each year an additional 146 million new souls come into existence— 45 million of them beyond any contact with Christians.

No Contact, No Mission

A fundamental flaw in today's Christian world mission is that most mission agencies are not targeting World A. They are targeting other Christians. No contact, no mission. These are the facts of the matter:

— 23% of the globe (World A) is ignorant of Christianity, Christ, and the Gospel.
— 97% of all Christians is out of contact with non-Christians.
— 90% of all evangelism is not directed at non-Christians but at Christians.
— 91% of all foreign missionaries is targeting populations in World C, the Christian world.
— 95% of all Christian activity benefits only World C.
— 99% of all Christian discussion and writing addresses only Christian interests.
— 99% of the Christian world's income is spent on itself.

Global Warming Reduces Contact

Mission in the 1990s is being pushed further out of contact with World A by a whole range of secular crises. One is the gradual increase in the earth's temperature of 0.3°C per decade predicted by the United Nations IPCC (Intergovernmental Panel on Climate Change). This will barely inconvenience air-conditioned Christians in World C. But experts predict that global warming will hit hardest the 2.4 billion who live in poverty by forcing them downwards into absolute poverty.

In 1980, the absolutely poor numbered 975 million (22.3% of the world). By 1991 this has risen to 23.4%. It is now calculated that global warming will speed up this process until by the year A.D. 2050 some 50% of the world will be living in absolute poverty. The unevangelized of World A will be at the bottom of that heap.

If mission in the 1990s can massively redeploy its resources into direct contact with World A, it could recover its traditional vitality. Otherwise, it will remain virtually irrelevant in the unfolding global drama.

METHODOLOGICAL NOTES ON TABLE (referring to numbered lines on opposite page). Indented categories form part of, and are included in, unindented categories above them. Definitions of categories are as given and explained in *World Christian Encyclopedia* (1982), with additional data and explanations as below. The analytical trichotomy of Worlds A,B,C is expounded, through 33 global diagrams, in a new handbook of global statistics: *Our Globe and How to Reach It: Seeing the World Evangelized by AD 2000 and Beyond* (D. B. Barrett & T. M. Johnson, Birmingham, Ala.: New Hope, 1990).
9. Widest definition: professing Christians plus secret believers, which equals affiliated (church members) plus nominal Christians. World C is the world of all who individually are Christians.
19. Total of all non-Christians (sum of rows 10–18

above, plus in 1991 some 210 million adherents of other minor religions). This is also the definition of World A (the unevangelized) plus World B (evangelized non-Christians).
23. Church members involved in the Pentecostal/ Charismatic Renewal. Totals on this line overlap with those on lines 26–32.
25. World totals of current long-term trend for all confessions. (See *Our Globe and How to Reach It,* Global Diagram 5.)
26–32. The total of these entries can be reconciled to line No. 9 by referring to *WCE,* Global Table 4.
48–54. Defined as in article "Silver and Gold Have I None," in *International Bulletin of Missionary Research,* October 1983, page 150.
53. Amounts embezzled (U.S. dollar equivalents, per year).

55. Total general-purpose computers and word processors owned by churches, agencies, groups, and individual Christians.
56. On strict UNESCO definition of book (over 49 pages).
63. Total of audiences in line Nos. 64 and 65, excluding overlap.
65. Total regular audience for Christian programs over secular or commercial stations.
71–72. (also 70). Defined as in *WCE,* parts 3,5,6, and 9.
74. Grand total of all distinct plans and proposals for accomplishing world evangelization made by Christians since A.D. 30. (See Barrett and Reapsome, *Seven Hundred Plans to Evangelize the World: The Rise of a Global Evangelization Movement,* New Hope, 1988).

STATUS OF GLOBAL MISSION, 1991, IN CONTEXT OF 20TH CENTURY

Year:	1900	1970	1980	1991	2000
WORLD POPULATION					
1. Total population	1,619,886,800	3,610,034,400	4,373,917,500	5,384,575,000	6,251,055,000
2. Urban dwellers	232,694,900	1,354,237,000	1,797,479,000	2,320,752,000	2,916,501,000
3. Rural dwellers	1,387,191,900	2,255,797,400	2,576,438,500	3,063,823,000	3,334,554,000
4. Adult population	1,025,938,000	2,245,227,300	2,698,396,900	3,300,518,000	3,808,564,300
5. Literates	286,705,000	1,437,761,900	1,774,002,700	2,257,853,000	2,697,595,100
6. Nonliterates	739,233,000	807,465,400	924,394,200	1,042,665,000	1,110,969,200
WORLDWIDE EXPANSION OF CITIES					
7. Metropolises (over 100,000 population)	400	2,400	2,700	3,500	4,200
8. Megacities (over 1 million population)	20	161	227	340	433
WORLD POPULATION BY RELIGION					
9. Christians (total all kinds) (=World C)	558,056,300	1,216,579,400	1,432,686,500	1,795,900,000	2,130,000,000
10. Muslims	200,102,200	550,919,000	722,956,500	961,423,280	1,200,653,000
11. Nonreligious	2,923,300	543,065,300	715,901,400	881,973,770	1,021,888,400
12. Hindus	203,033,300	465,784,800	582,749,900	720,736,540	859,252,300
13. Buddhists	127,159,000	231,672,200	273,715,600	326,923,760	359,092,100
14. Atheists	225,600	165,288,500	195,119,400	236,033,410	262,447,600
15. New-Religionists	5,910,000	76,443,100	96,021,800	119,656,570	138,263,800
16. Tribal religionists	106,339,600	88,077,400	89,963,500	99,535,190	100,535,900
17. Sikhs	2,960,600	10,612,200	14,244,400	18,720,690	23,831,700
18. Jews	12,269,800	15,185,900	16,938,200	17,865,180	19,173,600
19. Non-Christians (=Worlds A and B)	1,061,830,500	2,393,455,000	2,941,231,000	3,588,675,000	4,121,055,000
GLOBAL CHRISTIANITY					
20. Total Christians as % of world (=World C)	34.4	33.7	32.8	33.3	34.1
21. Affiliated church members	521,563,200	1,131,809,600	1,323,389,700	1,658,149,700	1,967,000,000
22. Practicing Christians	469,259,800	884,021,800	1,018,355,300	1,226,514,600	1,377,000,000
23. Pentecostals/Charismatics	3,700,000	72,600,000	158,000,000	391,638,700	562,526,000
24. Crypto-Christians (secret believers)	3,572,400	55,699,700	70,395,000	138,927,000	176,208,000
25. Average Christian martyrs per year	35,600	230,000	270,000	284,000	500,000
MEMBERSHIP BY ECCLESIASTICAL BLOC					
26. Anglicans	30,573,700	47,557,000	49,804,000	54,541,900	61,037,000
27. Catholics (non-Roman)	276,000	3,134,400	3,439,400	3,873,900	4,334,000
28. Marginal Protestants	927,600	10,830,200	14,077,500	18,858,300	24,106,000
29. Nonwhite indigenous Christians	7,743,100	58,702,000	82,181,100	149,851,200	204,100,000
30. Orthodox	115,897,700	143,402,500	160,737,900	181,547,200	199,819,000
31. Protestants	103,056,700	233,424,200	262,157,600	330,416,000	386,000,000
32. Roman Catholics	266,419,400	672,319,100	802,660,000	980,769,300	1,144,000,000
MEMBERSHIP BY CONTINENT					
33. Africa	8,756,400	115,924,200	164,571,000	240,339,600	323,914,900
34. East Asia	1,763,000	10,050,200	16,149,600	88,810,300	128,000,000
35. Europe	273,788,400	397,108,700	403,177,600	408,698,300	411,448,700
36. Latin America	60,025,100	262,027,800	340,978,600	449,253,200	555,486,000
37. Northern America	59,569,700	169,246,900	178,892,500	190,640,900	201,265,200
38. Oceania	4,311,400	14,669,400	16,160,600	18,501,500	21,361,500
39. South Asia	16,347,200	76,770,200	106,733,200	147,406,000	185,476,700
40. USSR	97,002,000	86,012,300	96,726,500	108,663,400	118,101,000
CHRISTIAN ORGANIZATIONS					
41. Service agencies	1,500	14,100	17,500	21,300	24,000
42. Foreign-mission sending agencies	600	2,200	3,100	4,050	4,800
43. Institutions	9,500	80,500	91,000	99,580	103,000
CHRISTIAN WORKERS					
44. Nationals (all denominations)	1,050,000	2,350,000	2,950,000	3,980,700	4,500,000
45. Pentecostal/Charismatic national workers	2,000	237,300	420,000	954,300	1,133,000
46. Aliens (foreign missionaries)	62,000	240,000	249,000	296,700	400,000
47. Pentecostal/Charismatic foreign missionaries	100	3,790	34,600	93,600	167,000
CHRISTIAN FINANCE (in U.S. $, per year)					
48. Personal income of church members	270 billion	4,100 billion	5,878 billion	9,320 billion	12,700 billion
49. Personal income of Pentecostals/Charismatics	250,000,000	157 billion	395 billion	1,059 billion	1,550 billion
50. Giving to Christian causes	8 billion	70 billion	100.3 billion	163 billion	220 billion
51. Churches' income	7 billion	50 billion	64.5 billion	85 billion	100 billion
52. Parachurch and institutional income	1 billion	20 billion	35.8 billion	78 billion	120 billion
53. Ecclesiastical crime	300,000	5,000,000	30,000,000	987 million	2 billion
54. Income of global foreign missions	200,000,000	3.0 billion	5.0 billion	8.9 billion	12 billion
55. Computers in Christian use (total numbers)	0	1,000	3,000,000	82,600,000	340,000,000
CHRISTIAN LITERATURE					
56. New commercial book titles per year	2,200	17,100	18,800	22,600	25,000
57. New titles including devotional	3,100	52,000	60,000	66,500	75,000
58. Christian periodicals	3,500	23,000	22,500	24,900	35,000
59. New books/articles on evangelization per year	500	3,100	7,500	11,500	16,000
SCRIPTURE DISTRIBUTION (all sources)					
60. Bibles per year	5,452,600	25,000,000	36,800,000	53,269,000	70,000,000
61. New Testaments per year	7,300,000	45,000,000	57,500,000	80,178,000	110,000,000
CHRISTIAN BROADCASTING					
62. Christian radio/TV stations	0	1,230	1,450	2,340	4,000
63. Total monthly listeners/viewers	0	750,000,000	990,474,400	1,447,658,000	2,150,000,000
64. for Christian stations	0	150,000,000	291,810,500	466,673,000	600,000,000
65. for secular stations	0	650,000,000	834,068,900	1,221,037,000	1,810,000,000
CHRISTIAN URBAN MISSION					
66. Non-Christian megacities	5	65	95	155	202
67. New non-Christian urban dwellers per day	5,200	51,100	69,300	102,800	140,000
68. Urban Christians	159,600,000	660,800,000	844,600,000	1,124,611,700	1,393,700,000
69. Urban Christians as % of urban dwellers	68.6	48.8	47.0	48.5	47.8
70. Evangelized urban dwellers, %	72.0	80.0	83.0	88.0	91.0
WORLD EVANGELIZATION					
71. Unevangelized population (=World A)	788,159,000	1,391,956,000	1,380,576,000	1,231,183,000	1,038,819,000
72. Unevangelized as % of world	48.7	38.6	31.6	22.9	16.6
73. Unreached peoples (with no churches)	3,500	1,300	700	425	200
74. World evangelization plans since AD 30	250	510	620	959	1,400

Christian Mission and Religious Pluralism: A Selected Bibliography of 175 Books in English, 1970–1990

Gerald H. Anderson

There has been an avalanche of literature in recent years, both in books and periodicals, on the subject of religious pluralism. Out of the vast literature this bibliography is selected and limited on the following basis: it has the interests and concerns of Christian mission in mind, and it is limited to 175 titles, in English, published in the period 1970–1990.

For purposes of this study, we have expanded our scope to include the worldviews of Marxism and secularism. Multi-volume works are counted as a single entry. Due to space limitations, information on multiple publishers and annotations of the literature are not included.

Another bibliography of special interest and value is by Kenneth Cracknell, "Interfaith Dialogue and the Theology of Religion: A Selective Bibliography for Ministerial Formation," *Current Dialogue* (Geneva: World Council of Churches), 17 (December 1989): 32–43.

Unfortunately, there is no book in any language that provides a comprehensive study of Christian attitudes and approaches to people of other faiths throughout the history of Christianity. Such a study would be immensely valuable in light of the increasing interest and importance of studies in the theology of religions.

Contents

Bibliographies

Balchand, Asandas. *The Salvific Value of Non-Christian Religions According to Asian Christian Theologians Writing in Asian-Published Theological Journals, 1965–1970.* Manila, Philippines: East Asian Pastoral Institute, 1973.

Choquette, Diane, comp. *New Religious Movements in the United States and Canada: A Critical Assessment and Annotated Bibliography.* Westport, Conn.: Greenwood Press, 1985.

David, S. Immanuel, ed. *Christianity and the Encounter with Other Religions: A Select Bibliography.* Bangalore, India: United Theological College, 1988.

Elliott, Mark R., ed. *Christianity and Marxism Worldwide: An Annotated Bibliography.* Wheaton, Ill.: Wheaton College, Institute for the Study of Christianity and Marxism, 1988.

Mojzes, Paul. *Church and State in Postwar Eastern Europe: A Bibliographical Survey.* Westport, Conn.: Greenwood Press, 1987.

Pedersen, Paul D., ed. *Missions and Evangelism: A Bibliography Selected from the ATLA Religion Database.* Rev. ed. Chicago: American Theological Library Association, 1985.

Pruter, Karl. *Jewish Christians in the United States: A Bibliography.* New York: Garland Publishing, Inc., 1987.

Shermis, Michael. *Jewish-Christian Relations: An Annotated Bibliography and Resource Guide.* Bloomington, Ind.: Indiana Univ. Press, 1988.

Treesh, Erica, ed. *Cults, Sects, and New Religious Movements: A Bibliography Selected from the ATLA Religion Database.* Chicago: American Theological Library Association, 1985.

Turner, Harold W. *Bibliography of New Religious Movements in Primal Societies.* 5 vols. Boston: G. K. Hall; vol. 1: Black Africa, 1977; vol. 2: North America, 1978; vol. 3: Oceania, 1989; vol. 4: Europe and Asia, 1990; vol. 5: Latin America, 1990.

Union Theological Seminary in Virginia, The Library. *Christian Faith Amidst Religious Pluralism: An Introductory Bibliography.* Richmond, Va.: The Library, Union Theological Seminary, 1980.

Atlases

al Faruqi, Isma'il Ragi A., ed. *Historical Atlas of the Religions of the World.* New York: Macmillan, 1974.

Littell, Franklin H. *The Macmillan Atlas History of Christianity.* New York: Macmillan, 1976.

Reference Works

Barrett, David B., ed. *World Christian Encyclopedia: A Comparative Study of Churches and Religions in the Modern World,* A.D. 1900-2000. New York: Oxford Univ. Press, 1982.

Braybrooke, Marcus. *Inter-Faith Organizations, 1893–1979: An Historical Directory.* New York: Edwin Mellen Press, 1980.

Clark, Francis, ed. *Interfaith Directory.* New York: International Religious Foundation, 1987.

Crim, Keith, ed. *The Perennial Dictionary of World Religions.* San Francisco: Harper & Row, 1989. Originally published as *Abingdon Dictionary of Living Religions.* Nashville: Abingdon Press, 1981.

Draper, Edythe, ed. *The Almanac of the Christian World.* Wheaton, Ill.: Tyndale House Publishers, 1990.

Eliade, Mircea, ed. *Encyclopedia of Religion.* 16 vols. New York: Macmillan, 1987.

Ellwood, Robert S., and Partin, Harry B. *Religious and Spiritual Groups in America.* 2nd ed. Englewood Cliffs, N.J.: Prentice-Hall, 1988.

Klenicki, Leon, and Wigoder, Geoffrey, eds. *A Dictionary of the Jewish-Christian Dialogue.* Ramsey, N.J.: Paulist Press, 1984.

Lossky, Nicholas, et al, eds. *Dictionary of the Ecumenical Movement.* Geneva: World Council of Churches, 1990.

Melton, J. Gordon. *The Encyclopedia of American Religions.* 3rd ed. Detroit: Gale Research, 1989.

Neill, Stephen; Anderson, Gerald H.; and Goodwin, John, eds. *Concise Dictionary of the Christian World Mission.* Nashville: Abingdon Press, 1971.

Reese, William Lewis. *Dictionary of Philosophy and Religion: Eastern and Western Thought.* Atlantic Highlands, N.J.: Humanities Press, 1980.

Whaling, Frank, ed. *Religion in Today's World: The Religious Situation of the World from 1945 to the Present Day.* Edinburgh: T & T Clark, 1987.

Theology of Religions

Aldwinckle, Russell F. *Jesus—A Savior or the Savior? Religious Pluralism in Christian Perspective.* Macon, Ga.: Mercer Univ. Press, 1982.

Anderson, Gerald H., and Stransky, Thomas F., eds. *Christ's Lordship and Religious Pluralism.* Maryknoll, N.Y.: Orbis Books, 1981.

———, eds. *Faith Meets Faith.* Mission Trends, no. 5. Ramsey, N.J.: Paulist Press; and Grand Rapids, Mich.: Wm. B. Eerdmans Publishing Co., 1981.

Anderson, Norman. *Christianity and World Religions: The Challenge of Pluralism.* 2nd ed. Downers Grove, Ill.: InterVarsity Press, 1984.

Ariarajah. S. Wesley. *The Bible and People of Other Faiths.* Maryknoll, N.Y.: Orbis Books, 1989.

———, and Ucko, Hans, eds. *Religious Plurality: Theological Perspectives and Affirmations.* Geneva: World Council of Churches, 1990.

Barnes, Michael. *Christian Identity and Religious Pluralism: Religions in Conversation.* Nashville: Abingdon Press, 1989.

Bühlmann, Walbert. *God's Chosen Peoples.* Maryknoll, N.Y. Orbis Books, 1982.

———. *The Search for God: An Encounter with the Peoples and Religions of Asia.* Maryknoll, N.Y.: Orbis Books, 1980. (Published in England under the title *All Have the Same God.*)

Cobb, John B., Jr. *Christ in a Pluralistic Age.* Philadelphia: Westminster Press, 1975.

Coward, Harold. *Pluralism: Challenge to World Religions.* Maryknoll, N.Y.: Orbis Books, 1985.

Cox, Harvey. *Many Mansions: A Christian's Encounter with Other Faiths.* Boston: Beacon Press, 1988.

Cracknell, Kenneth. *Towards a New Relationship: Christians and People of Other Faith.* London: Epworth Press, 1986.

Cragg, Kenneth. *The Christ and the Faiths: Theology in Cross Reference.* Philadelphia: Westminster Press, 1986.

Davis, Charles. *Christ and the World Religions.* New York: Herder and Herder, 1971.

Dawe, Donald, and Carman, John, eds. *Christian Faith in a Religiously Plural World.* Maryknoll, N.Y.: Orbis Books, 1978.

D'Costa, Gavin. *John Hick's Theology of Religions: A Critical Evaluation.* Lanham, Maryland: University Press of America, 1987.

———. *Theology and Religious Pluralism: The Challenge of Other Religions.* Oxford: Basil Blackwell, 1986.

———, ed. *Christian Uniqueness Reconsidered: The Myth of a Pluralistic Theology of Religions.* Maryknoll, N.Y.: Orbis Books, 1990.

Drummond, Richard H. *Toward a New Age in Christian Theology.* Maryknoll, N.Y.: Orbis Books, 1985.

Fernando, Ajith. *The Christian's Attitude toward World Religions.* Wheaton, Ill.: Tyndale House, 1987.

Goldsmith, Martin. *What About Other Faiths?* London: Hodder & Stoughton, 1989.

Griffiths, Paul J., ed. *Christianity through Non-Christian Eyes.* Maryknoll, N.Y.: Orbis Books, 1990.

Hallencreutz, Carl F. *New Approaches to Men of Other Faiths, 1938–1968: A Theological Discussion.* Geneva: World Council of Churches, 1970.

Hamnett, Ian, ed. *Religious Pluralism and Unbelief: Studies Critical and Comparative.* New York: Routledge, 1990.

Heim, S. Mark. *Is Christ the Only Way? Christian Faith in a Pluralistic World.* Valley Forge, Pa.: Judson Press, 1985.

Hick, John. *God and the Universe of Faiths.* New York: St. Martin's Press, 1973.

———. *God Has Many Names: Britain's New Religious Pluralism.* London: Macmillan, 1980; Philadelphia: Westminster Press, 1982.

———. *An Interpretation of Religion: Human Responses to the Transcendent.* New Haven, Conn.: Yale Univ. Press, 1989.

———, and Hebblethwaite, Brian, eds. *Christianity and Other Religions: Selected Readings.* Philadelphia: Fortress Press, 1980.

Hick, John, and Knitter, Paul F., eds. *The Myth of Christian Uniqueness: Toward a Pluralistic Theology of Religions.* Maryknoll, N.Y.: Orbis Books, 1987.

Hillman, Eugene. *Many Paths: A Catholic Approach to Religious Pluralism.* Maryknoll, N.Y.: Orbis Books, 1989.

Hooker, Roger, and Lamb, Christopher. *Love the Stranger: Christian Ministry in Multi-Faith Areas.* London: SPCK, 1986.

Jathanna, Origin Vasantha. *The Decisiveness of the Christ-Event and the Universality of Christianity in a World of Religious Plurality.* Berne: Peter Lang, 1981.

Knitter, Paul F. *No Other Name? A Critical Survey of Christian Attitudes Toward the World Religions.* Maryknoll, N.Y.: Orbis Books, 1985.

Küng, Hans, and Moltmann, Jürgen, eds. *Christianity among World Religions.* Concilium, vol. 183. Edinburgh, Scotland: T & T Clark, 1986.

Martinson, Paul Varo. *A Theology of World Religions: Interpreting God, Self, and World in Semitic, Indian, and Chinese Thought.* Minneapolis: Augsburg Publishing House, 1987.

Neill, Stephen. *Christian Faith and Other Faiths.* Downers Grove, Ill.: InterVarsity Press, 1984. (Published in England under the title *Crises of Belief.*)

Newbigin, Lesslie. *The Gospel in a Pluralist Society.* Grand Rapids, Mich.: Wm. B. Eerdmans Publishing Co., 1989.

Oxtoby, Willard G. *The Meaning of Other Faiths.* Philadelphia: Westminster Press, 1983.

Panikkar, Raimundo. *The Trinity and the Religious Experience of Man.* Maryknoll, N.Y.: Orbis Books, 1973.

Philip, T. V. *Christianity and Religious Pluralism.* Bangalore, India: United Theological College, 1988.

Pieris, Aloysius. *An Asian Theology of Liberation.* Maryknoll, N.Y.: Orbis Books, 1988.

Placher, William C. *Unapologetic Theology: A Christian Voice in a Pluralistic Conversation.* Louisville, Kentucky: Westminster/John Knox Press, 1989.

Race, Alan. *Christians and Religious Pluralism: Patterns in the Christian Theology of Religions.* Maryknoll, N.Y.: Orbis Books, 1983.

Rajashekar, J. Paul, ed. *Religious Pluralism and Lutheran Theology.* Geneva: Lutheran World Federation, 1988.

Rupp, George. *Christologies and Cultures: Toward a Typology of Religious Worldviews.* The Hague: Mouton, 1974.

Samuel, Vinay, and Sugden, Chris, eds. *Sharing Jesus in the Two Thirds World: Evangelical Christologies from the Contexts of Poverty, Powerlessness and Religious Pluralism.* Grand Rapids, Mich.: Wm. B. Eerdmans Publishing Co., 1983.

Smith, Wilfred Cantwell. *Towards a World Theology: Faith and the Comparative History of Religion.* Philadelphia: Westminster Press, 1981; new ed., Maryknoll, N.Y.: Orbis Books, 1989.

Song, C. S. *The Compassionate God.* Maryknoll, N.Y.: Orbis Books, 1982.

Sookhdeo, Patrick, ed. *Jesus Christ the Only Way: Christian Responsibility in a Multicultural Society.* Exeter: Paternoster Press, 1978.

Swidler, Leonard, ed. *Toward a Universal Theology of Religion.* Maryknoll, N.Y.: Orbis Books, 1987.

Thomas, M. M. *Man and the Universe of Faiths.* Madras: Christian Literature Society, 1975.

———. *Risking Christ for Christ's Sake: Towards an Ecumenical Theology of*

Pluralism. Geneva: World Council of Churches, 1987.

Vroom, Hendrik M. *Religions and the Truth: Philosophical Reflections and Perspectives.* Grand Rapids, Mich.: Wm. B. Eerdmans Publishing Co., 1989.

Whaling, Frank. *Christian Theology and World Religions: A Global Approach.* Basingstoke, Hants.: Marshall Pickering, 1986.

Dialogue

Amaladoss, Michael. *Making All Things New: Dialogue, Pluralism, and Evangelization in Asia.* Maryknoll, N.Y.: Orbis Books, 1990.

Anglican Consultative Council. *Towards a Theology for Inter-Faith Dialogue.* 2nd ed. Cincinnati, Ohio: Forward Movement Publications, 1986.

Camps, Arnulf. *Partners in Dialogue: Christianity and Other World Religions.* Maryknoll, N.Y.: Orbis Books, 1983.

Christian, William A. *Doctrines of Religious Communities: A Philosophical Study.* New Haven, Conn.: Yale Univ. Press, 1987.

Cobb, John B., Jr.; Hellwig, Monika K.; Knitter, Paul F.; and Swidler, Leonard. *Death or Dialogue? From the Age of Monologue to the Age of Dialogue.* Philadelphia: Trinity Press International, 1990.

Fu, Charles Wei-hsun, and Spiegler, Gerhard E., eds. *Religious Issues and Interreligious Dialogues: An Analysis and Sourcebook of Developments Since 1945.* Westport, Conn.: Greenwood Press, 1989.

Gort, Jerald D., et al, eds. *Dialogue and Syncretism: An Interdisciplinary Approach.* Grand Rapids, Mich.: Wm. B. Eerdmans Publishing Co., 1990.

Hallencreutz, Carl F. *Dialogue and Community: Ecumenical Issues in Interreligious Relationships.* Geneva: World Council of Churches, 1977.

Hick, John, ed. *Truth and Dialogue in World Religions: Conflicting Truth-Claims.* Philadelphia: Fortress Press, 1981.

Küng, Hans, et al. *Christianity and the World Religions: Paths of Dialogue with Islam, Hinduism, and Buddhism.* Garden City, N.Y.: Doubleday, 1986.

Lochhead, David. *The Dialogical Imperative: A Christian Reflection on Interfaith Encounter.* Maryknoll, N.Y.: Orbis Books, 1988.

O'Neill, Maura. *Women Speaking, Women Listening: Women in Interreligious Dialogue.* Maryknoll, N.Y.: Orbis Books, 1990.

Panikkar, Raimundo. *The Intrareligious Dialogue.* Ramsey, N.J.: Paulist Press, 1978.

Rousseau, Richard W., ed. *Interreligious Dialogue: Facing the Next Frontier.* Montrose, Pa.: Ridge Row Press, 1981.

Samartha, Stanley J. *Courage for Dialogue: Ecumenical Issues in Inter-Religious Relationships.* Maryknoll, N.Y.: Orbis Books, 1982.

Sheard, Robert B. *Interreligious Dialogue in the Catholic Church Since Vatican II: An Historical and Theological Study.* Lewiston, N.Y.: Edwin Mellen Press, 1987.

Swidler, Leonard. *After the Absolute: The Dialogical Future of Religious Reflection.* Minneapolis: Augsburg-Fortress, 1990.

World Council of Churches. *Guidelines on Dialogue with People of Living Faiths and Ideologies.* Geneva: World Council of Churches, 1979.

Christianity and Buddhism

Cobb, John B., Jr. *Beyond Dialogue: Toward a Mutual Transformation of Christianity and Buddhism.* Philadelphia, Pa.: Westminster Press, 1982.

De Silva, Lynn A. *The Problem of the Self in Buddhism and Christianity.* New York: Macmillan, 1979.

Drummond, Richard H. *Gautama the Buddha: An Essay in Religious Understanding.* Grand Rapids, Mich.: Wm B. Eerdmans Publishing Co., 1974.

Keenan, John P. *The Meaning of Christ: A Mahayana Theology.* Maryknoll, N.Y.: Orbis Books, 1989.

Panikkar, Raimundo. *The Silence of God: The Answer of the Buddha.* Maryknoll, N.Y.: Orbis Books, 1989.

Pieris, Aloysius. *Love Meets Wisdom: A Christian Experience of Buddhism.* Maryknoll, N.Y.: Orbis Books, 1988.

Rupp, George. *Beyond Existentialism and Zen: Religion in a Pluralistic World.* New York: Oxford Univ. Press, 1979.

Swearer, Donald K. *Dialogue: The Key to Understanding Other Religions.* Philadelphia: Westminster Press, 1977.

Waldenfels, Hans. *Absolute Nothingness: Foundations for a Buddhist-Christian Dialogue.* New York: Paulist Press, 1976.

Christianity and Chinese Religions

Ching, Julia. *Confucianism and Christianity: A Comparative Study.* New York: Kodansha, 1977.

Covell, Ralph R. *Confucius, the Buddha, and Christ: A History of the Gospel in Chinese.* Maryknoll, N.Y.: Orbis Books, 1986.

Küng, Hans, and Ching, Julia. *Christianity and Chinese Religions.* New York: Doubleday, 1989.

Christianity and Hinduism

Coward, Harold, ed. *Hindu-Christian Dialogue: Perspectives and Encounters.* Maryknoll, N.Y.: Orbis Books, 1989.

Griffiths, Bede. *The Marriage of East and West.* London: Collins Fount, 1982.

Hooker, Roger H. *Themes in Hinduism and Christianity: A Comparative Study.* New York and Bern: Peter Lang, 1989.

Mattam, Joseph. *Land of the Trinity: A Study of Modern Christian Approaches to Hinduism.* Bangalore, India: Theological Publications in India, 1975.

Panikkar, Raimundo. *The Unknown Christ of Hinduism: Toward an Ecumenical Christophany.* Rev. ed. Maryknoll, N.Y.: Orbis Books, 1981.

Raj, Sunder. *The Confusion Called Conversion.* New Delhi: TRACI Publications, 1988.

Robinson, John A. *Truth is Two-Eyed.* Philadelphia: Westminster Press, 1979.

Samartha, Stanley J. *The Hindu Response to the Unbound Christ.* Madras, India: Christian Literature Society, 1974.

Sharpe, Eric. *Faith Meets Faith: Some Christian Attitudes to Hinduism in the Nineteenth and Twentieth Centuries.* London: SCM Press, 1977.

Thomas, M. M. *The Acknowledged Christ of the Indian Renaissance.* London: SCM Press, 1970.

Christianity and Islam

Brown, Stuart E. *The Nearest in Affection: Towards a Christian Understanding of Islam.* Geneva: World Council of Churches, 1990.

————, comp. *Meeting in Faith: Twenty Years of Christian-Muslim Conversations Sponsored by the World Council of Churches.* Geneva: World Council of Churches, 1989.

Cragg, Kenneth. *The Call of the Minaret.* Rev. ed. Maryknoll, N.Y.: Orbis Books, 1985.

————. *Muhammad and the Christian: A Question of Response.* Maryknoll, N.Y.: Orbis Books, 1984.

Goldsmith, Martin. *Islam and Christian Witness: Sharing the Faith with Muslims.* Downers Grove, Ill.: InterVarsity Press, 1982; rev. ed., Bromley, Kent: MARC Europe, 1987.

Kateregga, Badru D., and Shenk, David W. *Islam and Christianity: A Muslim and a Christian in Dialogue.* Rev. ed. Grand Rapids, Mich.: Wm. B. Eerdmans Publishing Co., 1981.

McCurry, Don M., ed. *The Gospel and Islam.* Monrovia, Calif.: MARC, World Vision International, 1979.

Muslim-Christian Research Group. *The Challenge of the Scriptures: The Bible and the Qur'an.* Maryknoll, N.Y.: Orbis Books, 1989.

Nazir-Ali, Michael. *Islam: A Christian Perspective.* Philadelphia: Westminster Press, 1983.

Parshall, Phil. *The Cross and the Crescent: Understanding the Muslim Mind and Heart.* Wheaton, Ill.: Tyndale House Publishers, 1989.

Rousseau, Richard W., ed. *Christianity and Islam: The Struggling Dialogue.* Montrose, Pa.: Ridge Row Press, 1985.

Vander Werff, Lyle L. *Christian Mission to Muslims: The Record. Anglican and Reformed Approaches in India and the Near East, 1800–1938.* South Pasadena, Calif.: William Carey Library, 1977.

Watt, W. Montgomery. *Islam and Christianity: A Contribution to Dialogue.* London: Routledge & Kegan Paul, 1983.

Wingate, Andrew. *Encounter in the Spirit: Muslim-Christian Meetings in Birmingham.* Geneva: World Council of Churches, 1988.

Woodberry, J. Dudley, ed. *Muslims and Christians on the Emmaus Road: Crucial Issues in Witness among Muslims.* Monrovia, Calif.: MARC/World Vision, 1989.

Christianity and Judaism

Brockway, Allan, et al, eds. *The Theology of the Churches and the Jewish People: Statements by the World Council of Churches and Its Member Churches.* Geneva: World Council of Churches, 1988.

Cohen, Martin A., and Croner, Helga, eds. *Christian Mission—Jewish Mission.* Ramsey, N.J.: Paulist Press, 1982.

Croner, Helga, ed. *Stepping Stones to Further Jewish-Christian Relations.* Mahwah, N.J.: Paulist Press, 1977.

———, ed. *More Stepping Stones to Jewish-Christian Relations: An Unabridged Collection of Christian Documents 1975–1983.* Mahwah, N.J.: Paulist Press, 1985.

De Ridder, Richard R. *My Heart's Desire for Israel: Reflections on Jewish-Christian Relationships and Evangelism Today.* Nutley, N.J.: Presbyterian & Reformed Publishing Co., 1974.

Fisher, Eugene J., et al, eds. *Twenty Years of Jewish-Catholic Relations.* Mahwah, N.J.: Paulist Press, 1986.

Flannery, Edward H. *The Anguish of the Jews: Twenty-Three Centuries of Antisemitism.* Rev. ed. Mahwah, N.J.: Paulist Press, 1985.

Fruchtenbaum, Arnold G. *Hebrew Christianity: Its Theology, History, and Philosophy.* Washington, D.C.: Canon Press, 1974.

International Catholic-Jewish Liaison Committee. *Fifteen Years of Catholic-Jewish Dialogue 1970–1985.* Vatican City: Libreria Editrice Vaticana, 1988.

McGarry, Michael B. *Christology After Auschwitz.* Ramsey, N.J.: Paulist Press, 1977.

Swidler, Leonard; Eron, Lewis; Sloyan, Gerard; and Dean, Lester. *Bursting the Bonds? A Jewish-Christian Dialogue on Jesus and Paul.* Maryknoll, N.Y.: Orbis Books, 1990.

Torrance, David W., ed. *The Witness of the Jews to God.* Edinburgh: Handsel Press, 1982.

Christianity and Marxism

Beeson, Trevor. *Discretion and Valour: Religious Conditions in Russia and Eastern Europe.* 2nd ed. Philadelphia: Fortress Press, 1982.

Bockmuehl, Klaus. *The Challenge of Marxism: A Christian Response.* Downers Grove, Illinois: InterVarsity Press, 1980.

Lochman, Jan Milic. *Encountering Marx: Bonds and Barriers between Christians and Marxists.* Philadelphia: Fortress Press, 1977.

McGovern, Arthur F. *Marxism: An American Christian Perspective.* Maryknoll, N.Y.: Orbis Books, 1980.

MacInnis, Donald E. *Religious Policy and Practice in China Today.* Maryknoll, N.Y.: Orbis Books, 1989.

McLellan, David. *Marxism and Religion: A Description and Assessment of the Marxist Critique of Christianity.* New York: Harper & Row, 1987.

Míguez Bonino, José. *Christians and Marxists: The Mutual Challenge to Revolution.* Grand Rapids, Mich.: Wm. B. Eerdmans Publishing Co., 1976.

Mojzes, Paul. *Christian Marxist Dialogue in Eastern Europe.* Minneapolis: Augsburg Publishing House, 1981.

Stumme, Wayne, ed. *Christians and the Many Faces of Marxism.* Minneapolis: Augsburg Press, 1984.

Christianity and New Religious Movements

Brockway, Allan R., and Rajashekar, J. Paul, eds. *New Religious Movements and the Churches.* Geneva: World Council of Churches, 1987.

Hexham, Irving, and Poewe, Karla. *Understanding Cults and New Religions.* Grand Rapids, Mich.: Wm. B. Eerdmans Publishing Co., 1986.

Melton, J. Gordon, and Moore, Robert L. *The Cult Experience: Responding to the New Religious Pluralism.* New York: Pilgrim Press, 1982.

Tucker, Ruth A. *Another Gospel: Alternative Religions and the New Age Movement.* Grand Rapids, Mich.: Zondervan Publishing House, 1989.

Walls, Andrew F., and Shenk, Wilbert R., eds. *Exploring New Religious Movements: Essays in Honour of Harold W. Turner.* Elkhart, Ind.: Mission Focus Publications (Box 370), 1990.

Christianity and Primal Religions

Burnett, David. *Unearthly Powers: A Christian Perspective on Primal and Folk Religions.* Eastbourne, East Sussex: MARC/Monarch Publications, 1988.

Donovan, Vincent. *Christianity Rediscovered: An Epistle from the Masai.* 2nd ed. Maryknoll, N.Y.: Orbis Books, 1982.

Éla, Jean-Marc. *My Faith as an African.* Maryknoll, N.Y.: Orbis Books, 1988.

Mbiti, John S. *New Testament Eschatology in an African Background: A Study of the Encounter between New Testament Theology and African Traditional Concepts.* London: Oxford Univ. Press, 1971; reprinted London: SPCK, 1978.

Oduyoye, Mercy Amba. *Hearing and Knowing: Theological Reflections on Christianity in Africa.* Maryknoll, N.Y.: Orbis Books, 1986.

Shorter, Aylward. *African Christian Theology: Adaptation or Incarnation?* Maryknoll, N.Y.: Orbis Books, 1977.

Taylor, John, B., ed. *Primal World-Views: Christian Involvement in Dialogue with Traditional Thought Forms.* Ibadan, Nigeria: Daystar Press, 1976.

Christianity and Secularism

Berger, Peter L. *The Heretical Imperative: Contemporary Possibilities of Religious Affirmation.* Garden City, N.Y.: Anchor Press/Doubleday, 1979.

Martin, David A. *The Dilemmas of Contemporary Religion.* New York: St. Martin's Press, 1978.

Neuhaus, Richard John, ed. *American Apostasy: The Triumph of "Other" Gospels.* Grand Rapids, Mich.: Wm. B. Eerdmans Publishing Co., 1989.

Newbigin, Lesslie. *Foolishness to the Greeks: The Gospel and Western Culture.* Grand Rapids, Mich.: Wm. B. Eerdmans Publishing Co., 1986.

Thomas, M. M. *The Secular Ideologies of India and the Secular Meaning of Christ.* Madras: Christian Literature Society, 1976.

150 Outstanding Books for Mission Studies

Selected by the Editors of the INTERNATIONAL BULLETIN OF MISSIONARY RESEARCH

Each year the editors of the INTERNATIONAL BULLETIN OF MISSIONARY RESEARCH select fifteen outstanding books in English for mission studies. Here are the 150 books selected from those published in 1980–1989.

Adeney, Miriam. *God's Foreign Policy.* Grand Rapids, Mich.: Wm. B. Eerdmans Publishing Co., 1984.

Anderson, Gerald H., ed. *Witnessing to the Kingdom: Melbourne and Beyond.* Maryknoll, N.Y.: Orbis Books, 1982.

_____, **and Stransky, Thomas F., eds.** *Mission Trends No. 5—"Faith Meets Faith."* Grand Rapids, Mich.: Wm. B. Eerdmans Publishing Co.; and Ramsey, N.J.: Paulist Press, 1981.

Arias, Mortimer. *Announcing the Reign of God: Evangelization and the Subversive Memory of Jesus.* Philadelphia: Fortress Press, 1984.

Arias, Esther, and Arias, Mortimer. *The Cry of My People: Out of Captivity in Latin America.* New York: Friendship Press, 1980.

Augsburger, David W. *Pastoral Counseling Across Cultures.* Philadelphia: Westminster Press, 1986.

Austin, Alvyn J. *Saving China: Canadian Missionaries in the Middle Kingdom, 1888–1959.* Toronto: Univ. of Toronto Press, 1986.

Axtell, James. *The Invasion Within: The Contest of Cultures in Colonial North America.* New York: Oxford Univ. Press, 1985.

Barnett, Suzanne Wilson, and Fairbank, John King, eds. *Christianity in China: Early Protestant Missionary Writings.* Cambridge, Mass.: Harvard Univ. Press, 1985.

Barrett, David B. *Cosmos, Chaos, and Gospel: A Chronology of World Evangelization from Creation to New Creation.* Birmingham, Alabama: New Hope, 1987.

_____, **ed.** *World Christian Encyclopedia: A Comparative Study of Churches and Religions in the Modern World, A.D. 1900-2000.* New York: Oxford Univ. Press, 1982.

_____, **and Reapsome, James W.** *Seven Hundred Plans to Evangelize the World: The Rise of a Global Evangelization Movement.* Birmingham, Alabama: New Hope, 1988.

Bassham, Rodger C. *Mission Theology: 1948–1975; Ecumenical, Evangelical and Roman Catholic.* Pasadena, Calif.: William Carey Library, 1980.

Beaver, R. Pierce. *American Protestant Women in World Mission: A History of the First Feminist Movement in North America.* Grand Rapids, Mich.: Wm. B. Eerdmans Publishing Co., 1980.

Berryman, Phillip. *Liberation Theology: Essential Facts about the Revolutionary Movement in Latin America and Beyond.* Oak Park, Illinois: Meyer Stone Books, 1987.

_____. *The Religious Roots of Rebellion: Christians in Central American Revolutions.* Maryknoll, N.Y.: Orbis Books, 1984.

Bosch, David J. *Witness to the World: The Christian Mission in Theological Perspective.* Atlanta: John Knox Press, 1980.

Boyack, Kenneth, ed. *Catholic Evangelization Today: A New Pentecost for the United States.* New York: Paulist Press, 1987.

Bria, Ion, ed. *Martyria/Mission: The Witness of the Orthodox Churches Today.* Geneva: World Council of Churches, 1980.

Brown, David. *All Their Splendour. World Faiths: A Way to Community.* London: Collins-Fount, 1982.

Brown, Robert McAfee. *Unexpected News: Reading the Bible with Third World Eyes.* Philadelphia: Westminster Press, 1984.

Bühlmann, Walbert. *The Church of the Future: A Model for the Year 2001.* Maryknoll, N.Y.: Orbis Books, 1986.

_____. *God's Chosen Peoples.* Maryknoll, N.Y.: Orbis Books, 1982.

_____. *The Search for God: An Encounter with the Peoples and Religions of Asia.* Maryknoll, N.Y.: Orbis Books, 1980.

Burgess, Stanley M., and McGee, Gary B., eds. *Dictionary of Pentecostal and Charismatic Movements.* Grand Rapids, Mich.: Zondervan Publishing House, 1988.

Cadorette, Curt. *From the Heart of the People: The Theology of Gustavo Gutiérrez.* Oak Park, Ill.: Meyer-Stone Books, 1988.

Camps, Arnulf, and Muller, Jean-Claude, eds. *The Sanskrit Grammar and Manuscripts of Father Heinrich Roth, S.J. (1620-1668).* Leiden: E. J. Brill, 1988.

Castro, Emilio. *Freedom in Mission: The Perspective of the Kingdom.* Geneva: World Council of Churches, 1985.

Clymer, Kenton J. *Protestant Missionaries in the Philippines, 1898–1916.* Urbana, Ill.: Univ. of Illinois Press, 1986.

Commission on World Mission and Evangelism. *Your Kingdom Come: Mission Perspectives. Report on the World Conference on Mission and Evangelism, Melbourne, Australia, 12–25 May 1980.* Geneva: World Council of Churches, 1981.

Conn, Harvie M. *A Clarified Vision for Urban Mission: Dispelling the Urban Stereotypes.* Grand Rapids, Mich.: Zondervan Publishing House, 1987.

_____. *Eternal Word and Changing Worlds: Theology, Anthropology, and Mission in Trialogue.* Grand Rapids, Mich.: Zondervan Publishing House, 1984.

Cook, Guillermo. *The Expectation of the Poor: Latin American Base Ecclesial Communities in Protestant Perspective.* Maryknoll, N.Y.: Orbis Books, 1985.

Costa, Ruy O., ed. *One Faith, Many Cultures: Inculturation, Indigenization, and Contextualization.* Maryknoll, N.Y.: Orbis Books; and Cambridge, Mass.: Boston Theological Institute, 1988.

Costas, Orlando E. *Christ Outside the Gate: Mission Beyond Christendom.* Maryknoll, N.Y.: Orbis Books, 1982.

_____. *Liberating News: A Theology of Contextual Evangelization.* Grand Rapids, Mich.: Wm. B. Eerdmans Publishing Co., 1989.

Covell, Ralph R. *Confucius, the Buddha, and Christ: A History of the Gospel in Chinese.* Maryknoll, N.Y.: Orbis Books, 1986.

Cragg, Kenneth. *The Christ and the Faiths.* Philadelphia: Westminster Press, 1987.

_____. *Muhammad and the Christian: A Question of Response.* Maryknoll, N.Y.: Orbis Books, 1984.

Crim, Keith, gen. ed. *Abingdon Dictionary of Living Religions.* Nashville: Abingdon, 1981. Reissued under the title *The Perennial Dictionary of World Religions.* San Francisco, Calif.: Harper & Row, 1989.

Dayton, Edward R., and Fraser, David A. *Planning Strategies for World Evangelization.* Grand Rapids, Mich.: Wm. B. Eerdmans Publishing Co., 1980. Rev. ed. 1990.

_____; **Wilson, Samuel; and Bakke, Raymond J., eds.,** *Unreached Peoples '82: Urban Peoples.* Elgin, Ill: David C. Cook Publishing Co., 1981.

De Gruchy, John W., and Villa-Vicencio, Charles, eds. *Apartheid is a Heresy.* Grand Rapids, Mich.: Wm. B. Eerdmans Publishing Co., 1983.

Dickson, Kwesi A. *Theology in Africa.* Maryknoll, N.Y.: Orbis Books, 1984.

Dillistone, F. W. *Into All the World. A Biography of Max Warren.* London: Hodder and Stoughton, 1980.

Drummond, Richard Henry. *Toward a New Age in Christian Theology.* Maryknoll, N.Y.: Orbis Books, 1985.

Dussel, Enrique. *A History of the Church in Latin America: Colonialism to Liberation, 1492–1979.* Grand Rapids, Mich.: Wm. B. Eerdmans Publishing Co., 1982.

Eerdmans Publishing Co. *Eerdmans' Handbook to the World's Religions.* Grand Rapids, Mich.: Wm. B. Eerdmans Publishing Co., 1982.

Elliston, Edgar J., ed. *Christian Relief and Development: Developing Workers for Effective Ministry.* Dallas: Word Publishing, 1989.

Ellwood, Douglas J. *Asian Christian Theology: Emerging Themes.* Philadelphia: Westminster Press, 1980.

Fabella, Virginia, and Torres, Sergio, eds. *Irruption of the Third World: Challenge to Theology.* Maryknoll, N.Y.: Orbis Books, 1983.

Forman, Charles W. *The Island Churches of the South Pacific: Emergence in the Twentieth Century.* Maryknoll, N.Y.: Orbis Books, 1982.

————. *The Voice of Many Waters: The Story of the Pacific Conference of Churches.* Suva, Fiji: Pacific Conference of Churches (P.O. Box 208), 1986.

Gilliland, Dean S. *Pauline Theology and Mission Practice.* Grand Rapids, Mich.: Baker Book House, 1983.

————, ed. *The Word Among Us: Contextualizing Theology for Today.* Dallas: Word Publishing, 1989.

Gittins, Anthony J. *Gifts and Strangers: Meeting the Challenge of Inculturation.* Mahwah, N.J.: Paulist Press, 1989.

Goodpasture, H. McKennie, ed. *Cross and Sword: An Eyewitness History of Christianity in Latin America.* Maryknoll, N.Y.: Orbis Books, 1989.

Greenway, Roger S., and Monsma, Timothy M. *Cities: Missions' New Frontier.* Grand Rapids, Mich.: Baker House, 1989.

Gutiérrez, Gustavo. *The Power of the Poor in History.* Maryknoll, N.Y.: Orbis Books, 1983.

Haight, Roger. *An Alternative Vision: An Interpretation of Liberation Theology.* New York: Paulist Press, 1985.

Hanks, Thomas D. *God So Loved the Third World: The Biblical Vocabulary of Oppression.* Maryknoll, N.Y.: Orbis Books, 1983.

Hansen, Holger Bernt. *Mission, Church and State in a Colonial Setting: Uganda 1890–1925.* New York: St. Martin's Press, 1985.

Henkel, Willi, ed. *Bibliografia Missionaria: Anno XLV (1981).* Vatican City: Urban Pontifical University, 1982.

Hesselgrave, David J. *Counselling Cross-Culturally: An Introduction to Theory and Practice for Christians.* Grand Rapids, Mich.: Baker Book House, 1984.

————. *Today's Choices for Tomorrow's Mission: An Evangelical Perspective on Trends and Issues in Missions.* Grand Rapids, Mich.: Zondervan Publishing House, 1988.

Hiebert, Paul G. *Anthropological Insights for Missionaries.* Grand Rapids, Mich.: Baker Book House, 1986.

————, and Hiebert, Frances. *Case Studies in Missions.* Grand Rapids, Mich.: Baker Book House, 1987.

Hill, Patricia R. *The World Their Household: The American Woman's Foreign Mission Movement and Cultural Transformation, 1870–1920.* Ann Arbor, Mich.: Univ. of Michigan Press, 1985.

Hooker, Roger, and Lamb, Christopher. *Love the Stranger: Ministry in Multi-Faith Areas.* London: SPCK, 1986.

Horner, Norman A. *A Guide to Christian Churches in the Middle East.* Elkhart, Ind.: Mission Focus Publications (Box 370), 1989.

Hunt, Everett N., Jr. *Protestant Pioneers in Korea.* Maryknoll, N.Y.: Orbis Books, 1980.

Hunter, Jane. *The Gospel of Gentility: American Women Missionaries in Turn-of-the-Century China.* New Haven, Conn.: Yale Univ. Press, 1984.

Hutchison, William R. *Errand to the World: American Protestant Thought and Foreign Missions.* Chicago: Univ. of Chicago Press, 1987.

Jacobs, Sylvia M., ed. *Black Americans and the Missionary Movement in Africa.* Westport, Conn.: Greenwood Press, 1982.

Jansen, Frank Kaleb, ed. *Target Earth: The Necessity of Diversity in a Holistic Perspective on World Mission.* Pasadena, Calif.: Global Mapping International, and Kailua-Kona, Hawaii: Univ. of the Nations, 1989.

Kane, J. Herbert. *The Christian World Mission Today and Tomorrow.* Grand Rapids, Mich.: Baker Book House, 1981.

Kang, Wi Jo. *Religion and Politics in Korea Under the Japanese Rule.* Lewiston, N.Y.: Edwin Mellen Press, 1987.

Kasdorf, Hans. *Christian Conversion in Context.* Scottdale, Pa.: Herald Press, 1980.

————, and Müller, Klaus W., eds. *Reflection and Projection: Missiology at the Threshold of 2001. Festschrift in Honor of George W. Peters.* Bad Liebenzell: Verlag der Liebenzeller Mission, 1988.

Keeley, Robin, ed. *Christianity in Today's World: An Eerdmans Handbook.* Grand Rapids, Mich.: Wm. B. Eerdmans Publishing Co., 1985.

Kinsler, F. Ross, ed. *Ministry by the People: Theological Education by Extension.* Maryknoll, N.Y.: Orbis Books, 1983.

Kirk, J. Andrew. *Liberation Theology: An Evangelical View from the Third World.* Atlanta: John Knox Press, 1980.

Knitter, Paul F. *No Other Name? A Critical Survey of Christian Attitudes Toward the World Religions.* Maryknoll, N.Y.: Orbis Books, 1985.

Koyama, Kosuke. *Mount Fuji and Mount Sinai: A Critique of Idols.* Maryknoll, N.Y.: Orbis Books, 1985.

Krass, Alfred C. *Evangelizing Neopagan North America.* Scottdale, Pa.: Herald Press, 1982.

Lausanne Committee for World Evangelization. *How Shall They Hear? Consultation on World Evangelization: Official Reference Volume, Thailand Reports.* London and Wheaton, Ill.: Lausanne Committee, 1984.

Luzbetak, Louis J. *The Church and Cultures: New Perspectives in Missiological Anthropology.* Maryknoll, N.Y.: Orbis Books, 1988.

Martinson, Paul Varo. *A Theology of World Religions.* Minneapolis: Augsburg Publishing House, 1987.

McGavran, Donald A. *Effective Evangelism: A Theological Mandate.* Phillipsburg, N.J.: Presbyterian and Reformed Publishing Co., 1988.

McGee, Gary B. *"This Gospel Shall be Preached": A History and Theology of Assemblies of God Foreign Missions to 1959.* Springfield, Mo.: Gospel Publishing House, 1986.

————. *"This Gospel Shall Be Preached": A History and Theology of Assemblies of God Foreign Missions Since 1959. Volume 2.* Springfield, Mo.: Gospel Publishing House, 1989.

MacInnis, Donald E. *Religion in China Today: Policy and Practice.* Maryknoll, N.Y.: Orbis Books, 1989.

McLoughlin, William G. *Cherokees and Missionaries, 1789–1839.* New Haven, Conn.: Yale Univ. Press. 1984.

Meeking, Basil, and Stott, John R., eds. *The Evangelical-Roman Catholic Dialogue on Mission: 1977–1984.* Grand Rapids, Mich.: Wm. B. Eerdmans Publishing Co., 1986.

Míguez Bonino, José. *Toward a Christian Political Ethics.* Philadelphia: Fortress Press, 1983.

Motte, Mary, and Lang, Joseph R., eds. *Mission in Dialogue: The SEDOS Research Seminar on the Future of Mission.* Maryknoll, N.Y.: Orbis Books, 1982.

Murray, Jocelyn. *Proclaim the Good News: A Short History of the Church Missionary Society.* London: Hodder and Stoughton, 1985.

Neill, Stephen. *A History of Christianity in India: The Beginnings to A.D. 1707.* London: Cambridge Univ. Press. 1984.

————. *A History of Christianity in India: 1707–1858.* New York: Cambridge Univ. Press. 1986.

Nemer, Lawrence. *Anglican and Roman Catholic Attitudes on Missions: An Historical Study of Two English Missionary Societies in the Late Nineteenth Century (1865–1885).* St. Augustin, West Germany: Steyler Verlag, 1982.

Newbigin, Lesslie. *Foolishness to the Greeks: The Gospel and Western Culture.* Grand Rapids, Mich.: Wm. B. Eerdmans Publishing Co., 1986.

————. *The Gospel in a Pluralist Society.* Grand Rapids, Mich.: Wm. B. Eerdmans Publishing Co., and Geneva: World Council of Churches, 1989.

Nicholls, Bruce, ed. *In Word and Deed: Evangelism and Social Responsibility.* Grand Rapids, Mich.: Wm. B. Eerdmans Publishing Co., 1986.

Nida, Eugene A., and Reyburn, William D. *Meaning Across Cultures.* Maryknoll, N.Y.: Orbis Books, 1981.

Nouwen, Henri J. M. *Gracias! A Latin American Journal.* New York: Harper & Row, 1983.

Padilla, C. René. *Mission Between the Times.* Grand Rapids, Mich.: Wm. B. Eerdmans Publishing Co., 1985.

Pate, Larry D. *From Every People: A Handbook of Two-Thirds World Missions with Directory, Histories, Analysis.* Monrovia, Calif.: MARC/World Vision International, 1989.

Phillips, James M. *From the Rising of the Sun. Christians and Society in Contemporary Japan.* Maryknoll, N.Y.: Orbis Books, 1981.

Roberts, W. Dayton, and Siewert, John A., eds. *Mission Handbook: Canada/USA Protestant Ministries Overseas. 14th edition.* Monrovia, Calif.: MARC/World Vision International, and Grand Rapids, Mich.: Zondervan Publishing House, 1989.

Russell, Letty, M., et al, eds. *Inheriting Our Mothers' Gardens: Feminist Theology in Third World Perspective.* Philadelphia: Westminster Press, 1988.

Samartha, Stanley J. *Courage for Dialogue: Ecumenical Issues in Inter-religious Relationships.* Geneva: World Council of Churches: and Maryknoll, N.Y.: Orbis Books, 1981.

Samuel, Vinay, and Sugden, Chris, eds. *Sharing Jesus in the Two Thirds World.* Grand Rapids, Mich.: Wm. B. Eerdmans Publishing Co., 1984.

Sanneh, Lamin. *West African Christianity: The Religious Impact.* Maryknoll, N.Y.: Orbis Books, 1983.

————. *Translating the Message: The Missionary Impact on Culture.* Maryknoll, N.Y.: Orbis Books, 1989.

Sawatsky, Walter. *Soviet Evangelicals Since World War II.* Scottdale, Pa.: Herald Press, 1981.

Scherer, James A. *Gospel, Church, and Kingdom: Comparative Studies in World Mission Theology.* Minneapolis: Augsburg Publishing House, 1987.

————. *That the Gospel May be Sincerely Preached Throughout the World: A Lutheran Perspective on Mission and Evangelism in the 20th Century.* New York and Geneva: Lutheran World Federation, 1983.

Schreck, Harley, and Barrett, David, eds. *Unreached Peoples: Clarifying the Task.* Pasadena, Calif.: MARC/World Vision, 1987.

Schreiter, Robert J. *Constructing Local Theologies.* Maryknoll, N.Y.: Orbis Books, 1985.

Schurhammer, Georg. *Francis Xavier: His Life, His Times. Volume III: Indonesia and India (1545–1549).* Rome: The Jesuit Historical Institute, 1980.

Scott, Waldron. *Bring Forth Justice: A Contemporary Perspective on Mission.* Grand Rapids, Mich.: Wm. B. Eerdmans Publishing Co., 1980.

Senior, Donald, and Stuhmueller, Carroll. *The Biblical Foundations for Mission.* Maryknoll, N.Y.: Orbis Books, 1983.

Sharpe, Eric J. *Karl Ludvig Reichelt: Missionary, Scholar and Pilgrim.* Hong Kong: Tao Fong Shan Ecumenical Centre (Shatin, N.T.), 1984.

Shenk, Wilbert R., ed. *Exploring Church Growth.* Grand Rapids, Mich.: Wm. B. Eerdmans Publishing Co., 1983.

Sider, Ronald J., ed. *Evangelicals and Development: Toward a Theology of Social Change.* Philadelphia: Westminster Press, 1982.

Smith, Wilfred Cantwell. *Towards a World Theology: Faith and the Comparative History of Religion.* Philadelphia, Pa.: Westminster Press, 1981.

Sobrino, Jon. *Jesus in Latin America.* Maryknoll, N.Y.: Orbis Books, 1987.

Spykman, Gordon, et al. *Let My People Live: Faith and Struggle in Central America.* Grand Rapids, Mich.: Wm. B. Eerdmans Publishing Co., 1988.

Stackhouse, Max L., et al. *Apologia: Contextualization, Globalization, and Mission in Theological Education.* Grand Rapids, Mich.: Wm. B. Eerdmans Publishing Co., 1988.

Stamoolis, James J. *Eastern Orthodox Mission Theology Today.* Maryknoll, N.Y.: Orbis Books, 1986.

Starling, Allan, ed. *Seeds of Promise: World Consultation on Frontier Missions, Edinburgh '80.* Pasadena, Calif.: William Carey Library, 1981.

Stevens Arroyo, Antonio M. *Prophets Denied Honor: An Anthology on the Hispano Church of the United States.* Maryknoll, N.Y.: Orbis Books, 1980.

Tippett, Alan R. *Introduction to Missiology.* Pasadena, Calif.: William Carey Library, 1987.

Tucker, Ruth A. *Another Gospel: Alternative Religions and the New Age Movement.* Grand Rapids, Mich.: Zondervan Publishing House, 1989.

————. *Guardians of the Great Commission: The Story of Women in Modern Missions.* Grand Rapids, Mich.: Zondervan Publishing House, 1988.

————, and Liefeld, Walter L. *Daughters of the Church: Women and Ministry from New Testament Times to the Present.* Grand Rapids, Mich.: Zondervan Publishing House, 1987.

Tutu, Desmond. *Crying in the Wilderness: The Struggle for Justice in South Africa.* Grand Rapids, Mich.: Wm. B. Eerdmans Publishing Co., 1982.

————. *Hope and Suffering: Sermons and Speeches.* Grand Rapids, Mich.: Wm. B. Eerdmans Publishing Co., 1984.

Union Theological Seminary in Virginia. *Christian Faith Amidst Religious Pluralism: An Introductory Bibliography.* Richmond, Va.: The Library, Union Theological Seminary in Virginia, 1981.

Wagner, C. Peter. *Church Growth and the Whole Gospel: A Biblical Mandate.* San Francisco: Harper & Row, 1981.

————. *Strategies for Church Growth.* Ventura, Calif.: Regal Books, 1987.

Walshe, Peter, *Church versus State in South Africa: The Case of the Christian Institute.* Maryknoll, N.Y.: Orbis Books, 1983.

Webster, John C. B., and Webster, Ellen Low, eds. *The Church and Women in the Third World.* Philadelphia: Westminster Press, 1985.

Whaling, Frank, ed. *The World's Religious Traditions: Essays in honour of Wilfred Cantwell Smith.* Edinburgh, Scotland: T. & T. Clark, 1984.

Whiteman, Darrell. *Melanesians and Missionaries.* Pasadena, Calif.: William Carey Library, 1983.

Wickeri, Philip L. *Seeking the Common Ground: Protestant Christianity, the Three-Self Movement, and China's United Front.* Maryknoll, N.Y.: Orbis Books, 1988.

Wiest, Jean-Paul. *Maryknoll in China: A History, 1918–1955.* Armonk, N.Y.: M. E. Sharpe, 1988.

Wilson, Samuel, ed. *Mission Handbook: North American Protestant Ministries Overseas. 12th Edition.* Monrovia, Calif.: MARC/World Vision International, 1981.

————, and Siewert, John, eds. *Mission Handbook: North American Protestant Ministries Overseas. 13th Edition.* Monrovia, Calif.: MARC/World Vision, 1986.

Winter, Ralph D., and Hawthorne, Steven C., eds. *Perspectives on the World Christian Movement: A Reader.* Pasadena, Calif.: William Carey Library, 1981.